BEHIND THE CURTAIN OF COMMON SAYINGS

UNCOVERING THE SECRET HISTORY BEHIND IDIOMS AND THE ORIGINS OF WORDS AND PHRASES

BILL O'NEILL

ISBN: 978-1-64845-132-4

CONTENTS

DON'T FORGET:
TWO FREE BOOKS

GET THEM FOR FREE ON
WWW.TRIVIABILL.COM

INTRODUCTION

Do you know why we say that we're *cut to the quick*? If you think that the word *quick* might have something to do with being rapid there, then you can think again.

Or how about *cutting to the chase*? And why are things that are great or perform exceptionally well said to *cut the mustard*? Have you ever heard of someone *cutting the Gordian knot*? What on earth does that mean?

The English language is full of bizarre phrases and expressions like these, whose meanings we might know — so we can deploy them without thinking in everyday conversation! — but whose origins seem utterly mysterious or downright impossible to figure out. It is precisely these kinds of unusual idioms, expressions, words, and phrases that we're going to explore in this book.

This is *Behind the Curtain* — a guide to the fascinating origins of more than 100 English phrases and idioms. From *biting the bullet* to *eating crow*, and from *stealing someone's thunder* to *taking a raincheck*, we're going to take a whistle-stop journey through dozens of everyday phrases, tracking their meaning, history, and origins every step of the way.

For ease of reference, all the phrases we're looking at here are arranged in roughly alphabetical order, based on the most important word in each one: so, we're starting with the story of the *Achilles heel* and working our way through to the likes of *crying wolf* and *Pandora's box*.

1

Then, two final appendix sections will guide us through 15 of the most quintessentially American expressions you can imagine, which you'll rarely encounter outside of the United States, before we take one final look at a further set of 15 quintessentially British expressions—among them *taking a butcher's*, *pulling a blinder*, and *spending a penny*!

So, let's get this A-to-Z journey underway, shall we? And let's take a peek behind the curtain of our very first expression...

ACHILLES HEEL

When we say something is someone's *Achilles heel*, we mean that it is their one flaw or point of vulnerability — the only way that an otherwise seemingly untouchable or unbreakable person or thing can be harmed or brought down to Earth.

Achilles was a great legendary hero in Greek myth. The son of the mortal king Peleus and the sea nymph Thetis, he had both human and godly attributes, and through his noble birth, rose in power and status in the Trojan army of the great king Agamemnon.

Although tales and legends of Achilles' life vary, the most famous version of his story comes from the Greek writer Homer. According to his account, Achilles was raised by his mother at Phthia, in ancient Thessaly, alongside his childhood friend Patroclus, who later fought and died with him in the Trojan War. It is from a tale that emerged outside of Homer's *Iliad*, however, that gives us the *Achilles heel*.

According to the story, when he was still a baby, Achilles' mother Thetis used her powers to dip her infant son in the waters of the River Styx. The river made Achilles immortal and invulnerable to injury — but because Thetis held him by his foot, he retained a single vulnerable point on his ankle. Decades later, Achilles was slain in battle during the Trojan Wars when an arrow, shot by Paris, the lover of Helen of Troy, struck his foot: the one mortal point of his body.

This tale not only gave us the phrase *Achilles heel* but is also the origin of the *Achilles tendon* that connects the heelbone to the calf muscle.

BALLPARK FIGURE

The ballpark in the expression *ballpark figure* is, unsurprisingly, a baseball stadium. In fact, historically, the word *ballpark* has been used to describe an area for playing baseball since the late 1800s.

By the 1940s, however, midway through World War II and in the years leading up to the Space Race, the size and openness of a baseball ballpark gave the word a new life as a metaphor. It was used to refer to anywhere or anything—as seen from the cockpit or gun turret of an aircraft, for instance—that appeared as vast and as open as a baseball field. This meaning seems to have first emerged among American Air Force pilots and aeronautical engineers, who soon passed it on to their British Royal Air Force allies. Before long, the expression had slipped into use on both sides of the Atlantic.

It is from this sense of somewhere vast and open that a second metaphorical sense soon began to appear. First recorded in 1945, to be *in the ballpark* came to mean to be vaguely within an expected or appropriate range or limit. To be *in the right ballpark* or *in the same ballpark*, moreover, came to mean to be vaguely accurate, or at least within the right scope or area of meaning. And finally, by the 1960s, people were talking about *ballpark figures*—that is, figures or estimates that were only approximations but considered to be within an acceptable range.

JUMP ON THE BANDWAGON

When someone *jumps on a bandwagon*, they join up with an already ongoing trend or movement—often with the implication that, in doing so, they are behaving performatively or opportunistically. But what exactly is a *bandwagon*, and why would anyone want to *jump* on one?

Dating back to the mid-1800s, a *bandwagon* is quite literally that: a large wooden cart or wagon-like vehicle, sizeable enough to transport all the members of a band in a parade or procession. It was thanks to this image of a group of people, all working together with a single task or job in mind, that the word *bandwagon* soon came to be used more figuratively of anything that brings together like-minded people.

Toward the end of the 19th century, a political party or movement, a faction of supporters or campaigners, and all manner of disparate groups and "bands" were ultimately being labeled as "bandwagons." And from there, it took only another leap of imagination before people who were opportunistically lending their support to these kinds of causes were said to be "jumping" (or climbing or hopping) on the campaigners' bandwagon!

BASKET CASE

When we call someone a *basket case* today, we tend to mean something fairly flippant. They're dysfunctional, they're wildly incompetent, or they're so madcap and feather brained as to be totally unreliable, incapacitated, or only a moment away from total breakdown!

For such a comical-sounding and usually quite throwaway remark, however, this particular expression allegedly has a grim and rather unpleasant history.

The term *basket case* itself dates back to the early 1900s and first emerged in American journalistic accounts of World War I. In that original military context, the phrase is said by some to have referred to a fallen soldier on the battlefields of Europe whose injuries were so total that they — quite literally — had to be carried from the front line in a basket or wagon. Another twist on this sorry tale suggests that the basket was actually employed when the soldier returned home and had to be carried to his doorstep by military doctors. Either way, more often than not, it is said that this term once referred specifically to a soldier who had lost all four of their limbs in a shelling raid or some similar explosive attack.

Some historians and language experts have called that story into question, however, and today even the hallowed *Oxford English Dictionary* has labeled that tale as an "urban legend" with "little or no factual basis." If that is not this expression's true origin, then what is?

That is something of a mystery. The term was certainly used by wartime surgeons and doctors in their medical reports, but if they were not referring to soldiers suffering this level of debilitating injury, it is not clear precisely what they meant when they referred to the men in their care as *basket cases*. Whatever the original implication, a little over a century ago, the term gradually weakened and became less serious in meaning. In the 1940s, it was first used for something or someone that is wildly dysfunctional or beyond repair.

THE BEE'S KNEES

"That's the bee's knees!"

If you've ever heard that expression before, you'll know that it is used to describe something wildly impressive. But what exactly is so impressive about a bee's leg joints?

Well, unsurprisingly, this is not a phrase to be taken literally! In fact, *the bee's knees* was just one of an enormous number of phrases and expressions that emerged in the early 1900s as part of a peculiar trend in young people's slang.

Beginning around 1905—and lasting well into the 1920s and beyond—a craze emerged in slangy language for coining increasingly bizarre expressions of amazement or impressiveness, all based around the stock formula of *the X's Y*. So, as well as *the bee's knees*, people spoke of the likes of "the snail's ankles," "the ant's pants," "the elephant's adenoids," "the clam's garters," "the canary's tusks," "the snake's hips," and even "the owl's bowels." Clearly (not least given that canaries don't have tusks and snails certainly don't have ankles!) realism wasn't at the forefront of this wave of coinages. Instead, the entire point seems only to have been to invent snappy, jargonish, quirky-sounding expressions— and the more memorable and downright bizarre the better!

Although the majority of these snappy phrases didn't catch on, for whatever reason *the bee's knees* did—and has remained in use ever since. Perhaps just one other phrase from this era has stood the test of time: it's for precisely the same reason that you might still hear people say something is *the cat's pajamas* today!

THE BIG APPLE

Why is New York called the *Big Apple*? As unlikely as it sounds, it's all down to horse racing.

It was way back in the 1840s that the phrase *big apple* first emerged in American slang. Back then, it was always encountered inside the stock phrase "to get a big apple," which meant to be absolutely certain or confident of something or to say something with total assurance. From there, in the early 1900s, the phrase *big apple* began to be used more broadly, referring to something that was not just assured or certain, but absolutely first rate—the greatest or most reliable of its kind, or something to be admired, longed for, or much desired.

In this newer, broader sense, *big apple* next came to be particularly attached to the New York horse racing circuit, which in its early heyday in the 1920s was widely considered the pre-eminent circuit of the time. Once that connection had been established, however, it was only another year or two before the phrase *the Big Apple* began to be used not just for New York's race ground but for the entire city.

TO TURN A BLIND EYE

If you *turn a blind eye* to something, then you intentionally ignore it. It's a well-known expression in English today — and according to legend, has a remarkable connection to an equally well-known figure from history.

The story begins in the early 1800s. The Kingdom of Denmark had recently joined forces with several of its neighbors and Europe's superpowers — including Prussia, Russia, and Sweden — to form a vast bloc of allied nations. The aim of this new coalition was for the allies to mutually protect their own ships and shipping routes, and in doing so keep Britain, the most powerful naval nation in the world, out of the Baltic Sea.

Understandably, Britain was not happy. Not only did the creation of this new coalition seem like an act of hostility against British trade interests but Britain was also worried that this bloc might be coerced into allying with Napoleonic France, against which Britain was already engaged in a bloody and bitter war. As a result, in 1801, Britain entered into a brief war against Denmark, intending to break the coalition apart before Napoleon had the chance to take advantage of it.

The Danish capital, Copenhagen, became the focus of the British attack. The port was besieged by two large fleets of British vessels, each under the command of a renowned British admiral. One was Sir Hyde Parker, a 62-year-old elder statesman of the Navy with decades of wartime experience, and the other was a relative newcomer by the name of Lord Horatio Nelson.

The two men had vastly different approaches to naval warfare. Parker preferred a slower, more cautious approach to battle, while Nelson had a reputation for being far more bombastic. During the ensuing Siege of Copenhagen, Nelson was second in command and therefore answerable to Parker's orders, and when Nelson's approach to the battle saw him run three of his 12 ships aground in quick succession, Parker signaled to him from his flagship to retreat, before his entire fleet was lost.

When word reached Nelson of Parker's signal, however, Nelson is said to have raised his telescope to the eye in which he had been blinded in an earlier battle and joked that he could see no such signal. Deliberately ignoring Parker's order, Nelson continued to push hard into battle, eventually securing a British victory in typical uncompromising style.

The truth of this story remains debatable, but Nelson's actions that day have long been said to have inspired this expression referring to any similar act of intentionally ignoring something.

TO HAVE BLUE BLOOD

Why do we say that someone who is aristocratic or from the upper echelons of society has *blue blood* in their veins?

It's an expression that dates back to the early 1800s in English, but it was originally adopted from Spanish: *blue blood*, or *blue-blooded*, is the literal translation of an earlier Spanish expression, *sangre azul*. (Etymologically, incidentally, those words are also related to our words *sanguine* and *azure!*)

Historically, the phrase *sangre azul* was used in Spain to refer to the royal dynasties and ruling classes of the region as an expression of the supposed pureness of their bloodline. Blood is red, of course, but the phrase *blue blooded* likely emerged in reference to the many visible blue veins seen on the royals' skin due to their characteristic paleness. Having pallid skin has long been considered a sign of good breeding and aristocracy, as tanned skin was associated with working outdoors; having pale skin, ultimately, was a sign that you could afford a more sheltered and pampered life indoors!

ONCE IN A BLUE MOON

Although *once in a blue moon* is used to mean "only very occasionally," some people believe that the phrase *blue moon* might have originally been used to mean an absolute impossibility—in much the same way that we might say that something will happen "when pigs fly" when we mean that it will never truly come to pass. Then, in 1883, the enormous volcanic eruption of Krakatoa in western Indonesia threw so much ash and dust into the Earth's atmosphere that for many places around the world, the moon really *did* appear to have a bluish tinge at night. As a result, the meaning of the phrase *blue moon* changed from "an absolute impossibility" to "something that happens only occasionally."

It is a nice theory, certainly, but sadly the evidence to support the Krakatoa story behind this phrase is lacking. Instead, it seems that *blue moon* actually first meant a long time—perhaps based on the notion that the moon's occasional bluish appearance in the night sky is a somewhat rare occurrence. It was from there, ultimately, that a longer version of the phrase, *once in a blue moon*, first emerged in the 1830s.

As some amateur astronomers will no doubt know, however, a *blue moon* is also the name given to the second full moon of a calendar month.

Although most cycles of the moon align fairly well with the changes of the months, disparities between the length of the moon's cycle and the lengths of our calendar months mean that sometimes two full moons can fall in the same month. This happens roughly once every three years, and so some people believe that this astronomical name might have inspired the phrase instead. In fact, it is the other way around: these second full moons were likely named after the expression *blue moon* because they were so infrequent, not the other way around!

TO PASS THE BUCK

A buck can be a dollar bill, a male deer, or a dashing young man. In the expression *pass the buck*, however, it is none of those.

It is thought that this unusual phrase likely emerged in the American frontier lands in the 1800s in the context of games of poker. Supposedly, an item—more often than not a knife or some similar tool—was passed from one player to the next during a game to indicate whose turn it was to deal or place the first bet. At that time, it was fashionable for knives and blades to have handles made of deer antlers, or "buckhorn." As a result, the item that was "passed" to show who was in control of the next hand became known as the "buck."

From there, *to pass the buck* came to be used more broadly to mean to pass on any burden or responsibility to another person. *Buck passing*, likewise, is often used of a great chain of people all refusing to take responsibility for some troublesome issue, and therefore passing it on to one another. And a play on the original phrase, *the buck stops here*, emerged in the 1950s to imply that someone would take total responsibility for all problems. This final phrase was famously popularized by then-US president Harry Truman, who had a sign bearing the motto on his desk in the White House to show that all national responsibilities rested with him.

TO KICK THE BUCKET

Why do we say someone *kicks the bucket* when they die? The phrase was certainly once a literal one—referring to an actual kick on an actual bucket!—but many people who think they know where this saying comes from actually have the wrong "bucket" in mind!

One popular theory claims that this phrase alludes to a man destined to be hanged, standing on an upturned bucket that is then kicked from under him by an executioner. Unfortunately, there is little to no evidence associating this phrase with hanging, execution, or even suicide, so it seems unlikely that this was the original context.

Another popular explanation is that the bucket here is a pale of cool water by the bedside of a feverish patient, in which bandages and flannels could be soaked to cool them as they rested. If a patient's fever were eventually to worsen, they might accidentally "kick" their carer's bucket of water in a fit of ague before finally passing away. Again, however, there seems to be little evidence to back this theory up.

Instead, this phrase seems to be descended from a little-known use of the word *bucket* to mean a crossbeam—which emerged in English in the 16th century, having been adopted from French. This bucket would be just the kind of beam from which animals to be slaughtered would be hung in a butcher's market or meat market—and as the hapless creature was killed, its legs would thrash around and "kick the bucket" as the butcher went about his work.

TO BITE THE BULLET

When someone *bites the bullet*, they deal with or accept something unpleasant—often with the implication that they have long been putting it off!

As the word *bullet* might imply, this phrase originally had military connotations and referred to the practice of giving wounded soldiers a metal bullet to bite down on while often very brutal and painful surgeries were carried out on them in field hospitals—without the use of an anesthetic!

In that original and literal context, this phrase first appeared in the language in the 1780s. From there, its meaning widened slightly, and *biting the bullet* came to be used to mean behaving bravely, stoically, or with great courage and resolve—just like a solider accepting his fate. It was only somewhat later that the phrase's meaning shifted slightly again to today's usage, in reference to someone bracing themselves ahead of some unpleasant experience that can no longer be avoided!

THE STRAW THAT BROKE
THE CAMEL'S BACK

When we say that something is *the last straw*, we mean that it is the last burden or element of unpleasantness that makes an entire situation utterly unbearable. In that context, *the last straw* is a shorter version of the longer expression, *the straw that broke the camel's back*, which is likewise used in English to imply precisely the same situation of awfulness or dejectedness.

Expressions along similar lines as this one have apparently existed in our language since the 1600s, with one of the earliest being "the last feather that breaks the horse's back." How camels and straws came to replace horses and feathers is unclear, but the version that we tend to use in English today appears to have first emerged around the early 1800s.

No matter what form the phrase takes, however, the image here is a surprisingly literal one. In the sense of someone or something becoming impossibly and unbearably burdened, *the straw that broke the camel's back* refers to an animal being laden down with so much cargo that the addition of just one final minute extra weight—be it a feather or a single blade of straw— proves too much.

LOOSE CANNON

A *loose cannon* is a wildly and often dangerously unpredictable person. And this bizarre metaphoric expression has its roots in a similarly wildly dangerous item of weaponry!

Back when cannon fire was the weapon of choice on naval warships, a cannon that was not sufficiently or securely tied down in a storm or on rough seas could prove enormously dangerous, as it would roll unpredictably around the deck as the ship was tossed to and fro. Allusions to this metaphor have been in use in English since at least the late 1800s, but it wasn't until the 1900s that this phrase is thought to have caught on, having been popularized by then-US president Theodore Roosevelt. He was quoted as having once explained that he didn't want to be "the old cannon loose on the deck in the storm" —that is, behaving wildly and erratically and unable to be easily held back or controlled.

LET THE CAT OUT OF THE BAG

When you *let the cat out of the bag*, you make public a secret or divulge something that should have yet remained unknown.

Some people would have you believe that the "cat" in question here is not actually a furry feline, but the old cat-o'-nine-tails — a many-tailed whip or scourge once used to painfully thrash badly behaved or untrustworthy sailors in a form of brutal naval discipline. If the sailor in question was suspected of protecting his accomplices following some shady scheme on board a ship, a quick flog with the cat would be enough to have him quickly give in and instead reveal their names. "Letting the cat out of the bag" — that is, taking the dreaded whip from its sack in preparation for his punishment — was therefore often enough to have the hapless victim start to reveal his secrets.

As convincing as that theory is, however, the evidence from the language does not back it up. Instead, a more likely explanation is that this phrase refers to an actual cat — and has an unexpected connection to another English expression!

This second story alludes to customers at country markets purchasing livestock and other animals to take home with them. Someone purchasing a piglet from a somewhat unscrupulous vendor might become the hapless victim of an act of sleight of hand, with the vendor at the last minute swapping the highly valuable piglet for a not quite so highly prized cat! Only when they arrived home would the vendor's act of deception be revealed, with the customer quite literally letting the cat out of the bag.

Ultimately, it is this apparently genuine act of commercial chicanery that is not only the origin of *letting the cat out of the bag* but also the expression *a pig in a poke*—meaning something of which the true value or nature is obscured or deliberately hidden!

RAINING CATS AND DOGS

When it *rains cats and dogs*, it rains very heavily indeed.

Throughout history, there have been scores of reported cases of bizarre things falling from the sky during storms and tornados — from frogs and fish to worms, golf balls, and even blood! But no, this expression apparently does not refer to some curious episode from history when live animals fell from the sky.

In fact, no one is entirely sure why we say it *rains cats and dogs*, but some of the proposed theories are at least more plausible than others. One somewhat literal explanation is that heavy rain thundering down on the roof of an old home might be enough to cause any pet cats or dogs sleeping upstairs to run down to their owners, just like the rain pouring down from the sky. A more likely root of this phrase, however, suggests that it may, at least in part, have been based on a line by the great writer Jonathan Swift.

In 1710, Swift — who is best known today for his fantasy novel *Gulliver's Travels* — wrote a satirical poem in *Tatler* magazine decrying the state of London's River Fleet (the tributary of the Thames that now runs in an enclosed channel beneath the city's famous Fleet Street). When heavy rain falls in London, Swift wrote that it can be seen, "Sweeping from butchers stalls dung, guts, and blood, / Drown'd puppies, stinking sprats, all drench'd in mud, / Dead cats and turnip-tops come tumbling down the flood."

Back when Swift was writing, London was not a pleasant or hygienic place to be, and its rivers were even worse than the streets. Dead animals and waste from kitchens, houses, and businesses were simply thrown into or washed away by the water — and it is precisely these squalid conditions that Swift was decrying in his poem. He might not have explicitly used the phrase *raining cats and dogs*, but his grim image of dead or drowned animals being washed away by a torrent of water during a rainstorm was perhaps enough to create an indelible impression on readers' and Londoners' minds, and in turn, inspire this curious phrase.

TO CUT TO THE CHASE

When you *cut to the chase* of something, you come straight to the point of the matter—skipping out anything dull or unnecessary—and in doing so, get right down to the true nuts and bolts of a matter. But what is the "chase" we're talking about here? And what exactly are we "cutting"?

As this phrase might suggest, *cutting to the chase* is an expression we owe to the world of moviemaking. It emerged in the 1920s when silent movie makers would use exciting chase sequences to liven up their film, especially following a slower or less dramatic scene. By quite literally "cutting to the chase," the editors and directors of the silent era could maintain their audience's attention by skipping straight to a livelier part of the plot and omitting any further dull material.

From there, it was another two decades before the figurative use of *cut to the chase* we use today first emerged in the 1940s.

OLD CHESTNUT

Why do we call a tired, trite, much-used old joke an *old chestnut*?

Contrary to what some people might believe, this expression does not actually come from the use and hardiness of conkers, or horse chestnuts, which can be dried and varnished and kept in such a way that they—much like an old joke—stand the test of time. Instead, this expression apparently owes its existence to the world of London theatre.

In 1816, a play called *The Broken Sword* was staged at the Covent Garden Theatre in central London. The play—written by a London theatrical manager and playwright called William Dimond—was apparently adapted from, or at least in part based on, an earlier French stage play (though precisely where Dimond took the storyline from is unclear). Either way, the play featured a scene in which one character, a captain, begins to recount an anecdote about something he had seen while out walking in the woods, until one of the other characters butts in and completes the story for him with the line, "A chestnut!…Captain, this is the twenty-seventh time I have heard you relate this story!"

From that context, it is easy to see how the captain's story might have inspired a phrase that came to mean a tired-out joke or anecdote—though there is a slight problem.

The earliest record of *chestnut* or *old chestnut* in print in reference to a much-recited story dates from the 1880s, more than 60 years after Dimond's play was written! Although the play had some limited success, and for a time was staged in the United States as well as London, if this truly were the origin of the *old chestnut,* you might expect to find more evidence of it in those intervening six decades.

As unlikely as the lack of evidence might make it seem, however, with no other sensible origin story to tell, it appears Dimond's play is what gave us this expression.

AS RICH AS CROESUS

You might have heard the expression *as rich as Croesus* used to describe someone who is almost impossibly wealthy. But who exactly was Croesus?

The original King Croesus was a 6th-century leader of Ancient Lydia, a Greek-controlled region of what is now mainland Turkey. As king, Croesus oversaw a vast expansion of Lydian territory, eventually extending his realm across much of the modern-day Aegean coast of Turkey and even succeeding in conquering and claiming the strategically important city of Ephesus as his own. In doing so, he became enormously rich, and tales not only of his military prowess but also his wealth quickly turned into a legend in the ancient world.

One tale of Croesus' time as king claims that he was once visited by the great Athenian lawmaker Solon, who tried to convince the king of his belief that material wealth was not the key to lifelong happiness. In response, Croesus reportedly had Solon expelled from his court and returned to Greece. As good a tale as that is, however, Solon and Croesus are now known to have lived at very different periods in history, and so—like much of what we know of this ancient and impossibly rich king—it is nothing more than legend!

CROCODILE TEARS

Fake, insincere, or otherwise hypocritical tears are sometimes known as *crocodile tears*. This peculiar expression is surprisingly old, dating back as far as the mid-16th century—but the bizarre explanation behind it is even older.

Back in medieval times, a peculiar myth emerged among the writers of ancient bestiaries (guidebooks to legendary animals and plants) that the fearsome crocodile sheds tears of sadness as it kills and devours its prey.

Quite where this belief came from is unclear. Crocodiles do have tear-producing glands in their eyes, just like humans—and the fluid they produce helps to keep their eyes moist and stops them from drying out. Unlike us, however, crocodiles don't cry for any emotional reason! Perhaps, instead, some ancient explorer once saw a crocodile basking in the sun, with the water from its last swim gradually evaporating, leaving tear-like lines of dampness in between the channels and cracks of the scales around its eyes?

Whatever peculiar idea gave birth to the legend of the sorrowful crocodile, however, it was these medieval myths that gave rise to the expression *crocodile tears* in the mid-1500s.

AS THE CROW FLIES

"It's about two miles, as the crow flies," someone might say in reference to a singular, straight route between two points—and not necessarily a route that you, in a vehicle or on even foot, might be able to follow!

This bizarre expression dates back to the 1700s. In simple terms, it alludes to the ability of a bird to fly directly from point A to point B, and in doing so avoid any and all obstacles on the ground that might hinder a direct route. Quite why this phrase came to refer to crows in particular is unclear—but curiously, a straight route has also been known as *a crow road* since the 18th century.

That is an expression that appears to have emerged in Scotland (where it has also come to be associated with the unstoppable, headlong progress of a person's life toward death). Perhaps, then, there is some connection here between these two meanings—or else a more straightforward one, alluding to crows roosting or nesting in the trees alongside country roads and lanes.

TO CURRY FAVOR

Chances are the only context that you will ever have heard the word *curry* used is a culinary one!

In that sense, the word *curry* comes from a local Indian word thought to mean something blackened or burned, perhaps in reference to the toasting of spices or charring of vegetables involved in making a thick, spicy curry sauce. The curry in the peculiar expression *to curry favor* — meaning to ingratiate oneself with someone else — is, however, completely different.

In this context, *curry* is an old horse-keeping term, adopted into English from French in medieval times, meaning to comb or groom a horse's hair. As for the "favor" in *curry favor*, it too comes from a French source — but a rather more surprising one!

"Favor" in this context is a corruption of the French name, Fauvel, which was long used in medieval folk tales as a standard name for a chestnut or dun-colored horse. In one of these tales, in particular — a moral tale dating back to the 1300s at least! — a vain and scheming horse named Fauvel gradually works his way up through the upper levels of society until he, the horse, finds himself in a position of considerable power. There, he is fawned over by all the leaders of the local church and court. In an attempt to ingratiate themselves with their new leader, they groom and comb his hair as he resides in his palace.

So when you're *currying favor* with someone, you're actually "currying Fauvel"!

TO PUT ONE'S
FINGER IN THE DIKE

This bizarre expression is used to refer to a fast-acting attempt to stop a worsening problem or to control a situation before it gets out of hand.

You might have heard a fuller version of this expression, which specifically alludes to a "little Dutch boy" who put his finger in a dike. That's because this expression comes from a popular old folk story in which a young boy spots a crack in a dam, or dike, outside the city of Haarlem in the Netherlands. Fearing that the dam might break if the crack were to worsen, the boy plugs the hole with his finger and waits there all night until morning, when he is discovered by the people of the city who then proceed to mend the dike.

Although set in the Netherlands, this tale was likely invented in America and first appeared in print in a set of children's stories — *Hans Brinker, or The Silver Skates: A Story of Life in Holland* — by the US writer Mary Mapes Dodge in 1865. It does not appear to have been based on any existing Dutch folk story, and so Dodge likely invented both the tale and the character of The Little Dutch Boy herself. In doing so, she gave us a new phrase for stopping a troublesome situation in its tracks.

TO GO DUTCH

When we split a bill in a restaurant, why do we call it *going Dutch*?

Unfortunately, this phrase has nothing to do with the characteristic fairness or kindness of Dutch people. It actually comes from an even older and somewhat derogatory expression, a *Dutch treat*.

As two great naval powers on the coast of Europe's North Sea, England and the Netherlands were for many centuries considered enemies, and the two nations' long-lasting hostility came to be mirrored in the language too. Ultimately, labeling something as *Dutch* in English was for a long time seen as a mark of disrespect or indicative of a lack of quality. (It is for this reason, for instance, that bravery instilled by liquor rather than heart is known as *Dutch courage*!)

After the founding of the United States, this trend was carried across the Atlantic too. It was there that the expression *Dutch treat* first emerged sometime in the late 1800s to mean a treat in name only. That is to say, rather than a friend offering to buy you lunch in a restaurant as a treat, you end up having to pay your own way. And it is from there that *going Dutch* later came to refer to the act of splitting a bill.

WHITE ELEPHANT

This expression takes us back to Siam, the ancient royal kingdom that would eventually become modern-day Thailand.

Historically—and in some countries, still today—in much of central and southeast Asia, elephants were considered working animals and beasts of burden. As such, they were used in everything from farming to construction—much like horses in the farms and ranches of the West.

An albino or white elephant, however, was something different. It was considered sacred—and so it was never put to work but instead housed and kept in captivity. Having a captive elephant, however, was quite a responsibility, demanding considerable upkeep, food, fresh water, and space. So, although owning an albino elephant was something to be treasured, the day-to-day reality of keeping one often proved more troublesome than anything to be celebrated!

This, however, gave the ancient kings of Siam an idea. If there was a courtier in their employ whom they disliked and wished to get rid of, the king would supposedly gift him a white elephant. The courtier could not refuse, because ownership of such a creature was so greatly respected—but the king knew that the realities of owning the elephant would in due course financially ruin the courtier and lead to his disappearance from courtly society.

As a result, the phrase *white elephant* came to be used for any similar gift or possession that, in the long run, proves itself to be little more than a financial or personal burden.

THE ELEPHANT IN THE ROOM

For such a well-known and well-established phrase, it might be surprising to find that the phrase *elephant in the room* — meaning an obvious issue or problem that nobody present or involved in is currently addressing — has been reliably dated no further back than the mid-1980s.

The metaphorical image of an elephant (in the sense of something large and unavoidable) inside a room (where it could not possibly be ignored, other than intentionally!) has been used in various contexts and wordings since the mid-1900s. However, the expression *elephant in the room* itself was not popularized until 1984, when it was used as the title of a book dealing with the tricky subject of helping and educating the children of alcoholic parents. As the title of the book suggests, the parents' problems cannot be ignored if their children are to be raised successfully and appropriately.

From there, the phrase quickly entered into common usage and ever since has been used to refer to uncomfortable matters, that should not — but easily can — be ignored.

IT AIN'T OVER TILL
THE FAT LADY SINGS

It ain't over till it's over. Or, to put it another way, *it ain't over till the fat lady sings*.

Although the origins of this phrase are disputed, the most common explanation is that it refers to the final scene of the famous German composer Richard Wagner's operatic epic, *The Ring Cycle*.

The final part of *The Ring Cycle* is Wagner's "Götterdämmerung," or "Twilight of the Gods." It, in turn, concludes with a suitably grand finale in which the Valkyrie Brunnhilde—usually depicted as a large and strapping warrior woman—brings the performance to a close with a vast ten-minute operatic solo. And it is this epic ending to such a monumental work that is understandably believed to be what inspired the notion of something not being completely over until *"the fat lady sings."*

Although Wagner's opera premiered in Bayreuth, Germany, way back in 1876, the expression it inspires appears to have been coined in America sometime in the early 20th century.

GASLIGHTING

One of the buzzwords of the last few years has been the notion of *gaslighting* someone.

Often misused to mean simply misleading someone or telling them a falsehood, the word is more fully defined by the famous *Merriam-Webster Dictionary* as meaning "to psychologically manipulate" someone, typically over a long period of time. This manipulation, the dictionary explains, is so insidious and so prolonged that the person eventually "questions the validity of their own thoughts, perception of reality, or memories and experiences confusion...and doubts concerning their own emotional or mental stability."

The verb *gaslight* has only been used in this contemporary way for the past few decades, but its roots can be traced back almost a century.

In 1938, the British novelist and playwright Patrick Hamilton—perhaps best known for writing the play on which Alfred Hitchcock's real-time movie *Rope* was based—produced a play called *Gas Light*. Set in late Victorian England, the play tells the story of a devious husband gradually attempting to convince his wife that she is losing her mind.

Hamilton's play was then adapted for the cinema by director George Cukor in 1944, starring Charles Boyer, Ingrid Bergman, and a young Angela Lansbury in her Hollywood debut. The film was a box office success and went on to be nominated for seven

Academy Awards (with Bergman winning the Best Actress Oscar for her performance as the put-upon wife).

It is Cukor's movie that introduced the term *gaslighting* into common parlance, though it is only in the past few years that the term has truly taken off in the language.

EVERYTHING THEY
TOUCH TURNS TO GOLD

You might have heard said of someone who can seemingly do no wrong and appears always to succeed in any enterprise they undertake that *everything they touch turns to gold.*

You might also have heard the expression *the Midas touch,* used in much the same way. But who was Midas—and why did he have this "golden touch"?

Midas was a legendary king of Phrygia, an ancient kingdom in central Anatolia, a region in modern-day Turkey just south of the Black Sea, who ruled sometime around the 8th century BCE. According to Greek legend, in return for looking after his satyr companion Silenus, the Greek god Dionysus granted King Midas a single wish. Known for his greed (and for his foolishness), Midas asked that everything he touched should turn immediately to gold—thereby granting him untold and eternal wealth.

Before long, however, Midas' wish turned into a curse. He could no longer embrace his family, and he almost starved to death when all the food he picked up to eat turned to solid gold in his hands. Midas pleaded with Dionysus to undo the wish. In return, the god told him to bathe in the waters of the River Pactolus, after which he would be cured.

The presence of gold dust in the waters of the river still to this day is said to be the remains of King Midas' lavish yet shortsighted wish.

TO GILD THE LILY

If you *gild the lily*, you attempt to make something that is already impressive or beautiful even more showy — often with the added implication that doing so is pointless or ends up ruining the thing you are trying to improve.

Like a great many of our longest-standing sayings and idioms, *gilding* (i.e., gold covering) *the lily* is a phrase we owe to William Shakespeare — although the wording we have ended up with today is something of a mangling of his original line.

In the fourth act of his history play *King John*, Shakespeare wrote that, "To gild refined gold, to paint the lily...is wasteful and ridiculous excess." The image being conjured here is clearly the same as the one we know today, but for some reason, the two original metaphors — gilding gold and merely painting the lily — have been confused over time, giving us the phrase as we now know it.

TO CUT THE GORDIAN KNOT

You might have heard an intractable, all but impossible problem likened to the *Gordian knot*. Perhaps too, you might have heard of someone who attempts to solve such a problem with blunt, violent, or unthinkingly forceful means as *cutting the Gordian knot*. But what do these two curious expressions refer to?

The word *Gordian* itself derives from the name of a legendary king of Phrygia, in modern-day Turkey, known as Gordius. Once a mere peasant, Gordius founded a great city—known as Gordium in his honor—which flourished as the capital of Phrygia in the 8th and 9th centuries BCE and which he ruled over as its king. Never one to lose sight of his roots as a penniless peasant, however, King Gordius put his old peasant's cart on display in the center of the city and dedicated it to the leader of the gods, Zeus.

King Gordius fastened the yoke of his cart to a post in the city square using an immensely intricate knot, the end of which was hidden from view below coil after coil of rope. As the centuries passed, a legend emerged in the city claiming that whoever could undo King Gordius' knot would, like him, prove to be a great leader and would eventually conquer all of Asia.

In 333 BCE, the young Macedonian leader and warrior Alexander the Great arrived in Gordium and saw the ancient king's cart tied up with the so-called Gordian knot. And on hearing that whoever undid the knot would be destined to wield great power, Alexander unsheathed his sword and simply cut the knot in two.

TO HEAR SOMETHING
THROUGH THE GRAPEVINE

Why do we say that we hear clandestine gossip *through the grapevine*? The origins of this peculiar expression in fact lie in the early days of radio technology.

It was in 1844 that the American inventor Samuel Morse first demonstrated his new telegraphic system of transmitting messages when he sent a radio communication from Washington to Baltimore. The technology was truly groundbreaking at the time—but some people, and especially some rural communities, did not at first see the need for this kind of electronic communication.

As a result, around two decades later, the phrase *grapevine telegraph* had begun to be used in America to describe the kind of person-to-person network of communication that typically exists in small towns and rural communities. Precisely what the "grapevine" here is meant to refer to is debatable, however.

Some explanations claim that the phrase refers to the dense vegetation in and around these isolated communities. Others claim that it refers to the simple fruit-picking and farm-laboring jobs that many people in these rural towns and villages might once have been expected to have. A more plausible explanation, however, is that the phrase is metaphorical: these person-to-person telegraphic networks connect everyone through ties and lines of family, friendship, and community—with these family "lines" resembling the coiling tendrils of a vine.

IT'S ALL GREEK TO ME

"I didn't understand a word of it. *It's all Greek to me!*"

Greek is one of only a handful of major European languages that is not written in the Roman Latin script of our ABCs. As a result, to someone who has no prior knowledge of the Greek *alpha, beta, gamma* lettering system, a page of written Greek would appear almost entirely incomprehensible. For that reason, *"It's all Greek to me!"* has become a well-established expression in our language referring to something that seems beyond the realms of a person's comprehension.

But how did this phrase become so well established? Well, for that, we can once again thank William Shakespeare.

In his retelling of the life of Julius Caesar in 1601, Shakespeare wrote a scene in which two of the conspirators working against Caesar—Casca and Cassius—talk about the Roman senator Cicero. "Did Cicero say anything?" Cassius asks. "Ay," Casca responds, "he spoke Greek."

"Those that understood him," Cassius goes on to explain, "smiled at one another and shook their heads; but, for mine own part, it was Greek to me."

THE HAIR OF THE DOG

Most of us will have at some point felt a little worse for wear the day after drinking more than we should have. And most of us will have no doubt also heard that a handy way of getting over a hangover is to have one more drink the following day—a drink that is commonly known as *the hair of the dog*.

But where does this bizarre expression come from? Well, oddly, the idea of using a "dog" as a cure wasn't originally anything to do with overdrinking.

Historically, a common cure for someone who had been bitten by a dog was to wrap the bite wound in a poultice including some of the fur or hair from the dog that had done the bite. The idea of "using like to cure like" is a particularly ancient one in medieval medicine—and still underpins modern-day alternative medicines like homeopathy.

"The hair of the dog that bit you" ultimately became a proverbial cure for using some element of the thing that had caused you pain or had made you ill to make you better again. Consequently, it came to refer to the notion of drinking to alleviate a hangover!

TO HIT THE HAY

Back in the early 1900s, when this expression first began to emerge in American English, beds and mattresses were not stuffed with soft padding and cushioning springs, but typically contained pads of dry grasses and hay. For that reason, *"hitting the hay"* — or, in a later version of the same phrase, "hitting the sack" — came to refer to going to bed.

The phrase appears to have first been used in American slang and is recorded in written English from 1903. The use of *hay* or *the hay* to refer to bed, however, is recorded slightly earlier, showing that stuffing mattresses with grasses and other similar materials is a long-established practice.

TO BREAK THE ICE

When the expression *break the ice* first appeared in the language more than 500 years ago, it referred to the practice of quite literally breaking up the ice in frozen rivers, lakes, and seas to allow for the passage of ships and other vessels. It wasn't until the late 1500s that the phrase—now well-established in the language—began to be used metaphorically.

At first, *breaking the ice* appears to have essentially meant moving on from a deadlock or beginning work or action in an enterprise, perhaps after a period of inactivity. The even more figurative meaning we tend to imply today—that is, to break an awkward silence in conversation or to get to know someone you are unfamiliar with—did not appear until considerably later and was first recorded in the mid-17th century.

TO BURY THE HATCHET

When we end a long period of enmity or grievance, we are said to *bury the hatchet*. Unlike many of the phrases we're looking at in this book, this one was originally quite literal.

The phrase *bury the hatchet* has been recorded in English since the 1600s, but the practice it refers to is considerably older. According to many early accounts of Native American culture, in order to show the end of a disagreement or period of hostility between families or neighboring peoples, actual hatchets would be symbolically buried in the ground by the chiefs of the tribes involved to show that peace had been brokered.

Although this ritual certainly took place among the Native American peoples, the phrase was likely at least partly based on or inspired by an even earlier English metaphor, *to hang up one's hatchet*, which likewise meant to symbolically end a period of grievance. It has been in use in English since medieval times and is recorded as far back as the early 1300s — long before English speakers were even aware of the New World.

STRAIGHT FROM
THE HORSE'S MOUTH

To hear something *straight from the horse's mouth* is to hear it firsthand. But what on earth does this peculiar saying refer to?

Oddly, this is another phrase whose meaning and origins are actually quite literal. One of the ways to judge the age of a horse is by examining its teeth and the inside of its mouth. The better state a horse's teeth are in, the younger and healthier (and therefore more valuable a racer, breeder, or workhorse) it is likely to be.

The phrase *straight from the horse's mouth*, ultimately, alludes to someone interested in purchasing a horse—but who is worried that they might be getting conned into buying a horse that is far older than the vendor is letting on—getting all the accurate information they need, quite literally, from the horse itself!

INDIAN SUMMER

An Indian summer is a period of calm, dry, warm, summer-like weather occurring in late autumn—precisely at a time when wetter, colder, more blustery weather might be expected instead!

It is sometimes claimed that this phrase emerged during the colonial period of British rule in India, known as the British Raj. According to this theory, the phrase refers to the weather of the Indian subcontinent, which could be all but guaranteed to be warm and humid while back home in England it was wet and windy.

In fact, this phrase is recorded in North America far earlier than that—meaning that the "Indian" in question here is what we would now more fittingly call a Native American. Quite what the word is meant to imply here, however, is unclear.

One theory is that "Indian" here simply means unusual or exotic, in the sense that such unseasonable weather is far from what would be the norm toward the end of autumn. Another theory claims that back in the late 1700s, when this expression first emerged, the area where these warm, dry conditions were perhaps most noticeable was still under Native American control, as opposed to the colonial areas of America's east.

Whatever the underlying notion, the phrase quickly caught on in American English, before finding its way into British English in the 19th century. It has remained in use on both sides of the Atlantic ever since.

MAD AS A HATTER

It might be tempting to think that the Victorian children's author and poet Lewis Carroll is responsible for inventing this phrase, given that he invented the character Mad Hatter in his *Alice in Wonderland* stories. In fact, the notion of hat-makers being "mad" is far older than even Carroll's writing — and is rooted in a grim aspect of fashion history!

In the 18th and 19th centuries, hat-makers used to use several poisonous chemicals and compounds — including lead and even oxides of mercury — in their work. In particular, a chemical called mercuric nitrate was used to help stiffen the felt fabric the milliners used to make their hats.

Prolonged exposure to chemicals like this — breathing in the mercuric particles in their poorly ventilated workshops and studios — understandably had a terrible effect on the hat-makers' health and caused various tremors, tics, and other nervous problems. Some hatters even developed psychoses and other mental issues as a result of the toxic chemicals they used every day. Ultimately, the expression *mad as a hatter* emerged in the language to refer to someone who appeared to be suffering from these kinds of conditions — and, of course, led to the creation of one of Lewis Carroll's most famous characters.

NO MAN IS AN ISLAND

A popular motto of humanity and the ties that bind people, even in the toughest and most isolating of times, the phrase *no man is an island* is a direct quote from one of England's greatest poets.

John Donne was born in 1572. Born into a Catholic family in London, Donne later became a cleric in the Anglican church and went on to serve as the Dean of St. Paul's Cathedral in central London in 1621. Unsurprisingly given such a pious background, much of Donne's verse and metaphysical poetry, literary sermons, and other works of literature and writing deal with complex issues of faith and religion. And included among them is a series of 23 so-called "meditations" on life and death — written following Donne's own brush with death, having contracted a typhoid-like fever in 1623 — which he called his *Devotions upon Emergent Occasions*.

It was in the 17th of these *Devotions* that Donne wrote that, "No man is an island, entire of itself; every man is a piece of the continent, a part of the main." Thanks to the continued popularity of his work and poetry, the line has since become proverbial — as has another of the most famous lines from the same essay, *Devotion XVII*: "Therefore, never send to know for whom the bell tolls; it tolls for thee."

TO LICK INTO SHAPE

This is another phrase for which the genuine origin is based on an entirely ungenuine (and downright bizarre!) piece of folklore.

In medieval times, back when our knowledge of the natural world was not quite as complete as it is today, people believed that bear cubs were born as shapeless, formless lumps of flesh. It was then the mother bear's task to quite literally "lick" her offspring into shape, producing a fully developed bear cub.

Precisely where this bizarre belief first came from is unknown; perhaps it was based on nothing more than the enormous size discrepancy between the adult and her cub, or else a mistaken explanation for why a mother bear would spend so long licking her cub clean after it was born. As misguided as the folklore might have been, however, it seems to have survived for quite some time and is even alluded to by Shakespeare: in *Henry VI, Part 3*, the future king Richard III describes his deformed and hunch-backed body as like that of an "unlick'd bear-whelp."

THE LION'S SHARE

Lions feature in a number of English phrases and idioms, several of which—like *in the lion's paws*, *in the lion's den*, *a lion in one's path*, and *in the lion's mouth*—have Biblical origins among the proverbs and stories of the Old Testament.

The lion's share, meaning the larger or largest portion of something, is an expression just as old as these others—but rather than deriving from the Bible, it has its roots in Aesop's fables.

Said by some historians to have lived in the Ancient Greek state of Lydia sometime around the 6th century BCE, Aesop was a former slave whose moral tales or fables were among the best-known stories in European antiquity. In fact, his tales are so well and so widely known that many historians today believe one man could not possibly have been responsible for them all. Instead, like a Mother Goose–type character, Aesop was likely apocryphal and little more than a made-up name attached to a plethora of stories from all parts and periods of Ancient Greek tradition.

Whether its author was genuine or not, it is the fable of *The Lion's Share* that is the origin of this expression. Although several versions of this tale exist (under several different titles), most involve a group of lowly animals—typically a cow, a sheep, and a goat—who go hunting with a lion. When the time comes to portion out the shares of the hunt, however, the lion takes the majority of the partnership's haul, as he is the king. The moral of the tale, ultimately, is a proverbial warning against entering into an agreement or coalition with someone or something far more powerful than yourself!

TO NAIL YOUR
COLORS TO THE MAST

If you *nail your colors* (or *your flag*) *to the mast*, then you openly reveal your opinions or declare your allegiance to a particular belief or policy.

Although several different explanations of this phrase's origin exist, the most likely is that it derives from the world of naval battles.

During the Age of Sail, in the heat of battle at sea, it sometimes proved difficult to keep track of which ship was on which side. Ships would, of course, display the flags and "colors" of their particular allegiance, but amid cannon fire and smoke these signals could easily be shrouded, damaged, and even lost altogether.

The crew of a ship whose "colors" had been torn or knocked down from their rightful place, ultimately, might have little recourse but literally to nail the tattered flags to the mast of their ship so that the neighboring vessels in the water could see whose side they were on (and so not find themselves under friendly fire!).

Prominently displaying the flags in this way also stopped enemy vessels from wrongly believing that a ship had surrendered.

TO FACE THE MUSIC

For such a familiar expression, it might be surprising to find that no one is entirely sure why—when the time comes to face up to the consequences of our actions or confront something unpleasant or long put off—we say that we are going to *face the music*.

We might not know this phrase's origins for certain, but that's not to say that we don't have some theories. At least one explanation is that this phrase likely emerged in the theater and refers to an anxious performer walking onto the stage—to the sound of the orchestra playing below—and having to face a hostile audience or begin their act despite their nervousness.

Another theory is that this phrase comes from the military, where it was once customary to quite literally "drum" a soldier who had been dishonorably discharged from his service out of his regiment, to the sound of his fellow soldier's drumbeats. Or, along similar lines, perhaps the "music" in this expression is not actually music, but another example of military slang: since the 17th century at least, the sound of gunfire and fighting has been known as "music" to soldiers in the army, and so when "facing the music," perhaps it was time for a soldier to face the heat of battle.

Whatever this phrase's origins, it appears to have first emerged in American English sometime in the early 1800s.

TO CUT THE MUSTARD

If something or someone *cuts the mustard*, then they successfully or optimally meet expectations or achieve whatever was demanded of them.

The origin of this phrase is at least partly shrouded in mystery. We do know that, despite its similarity to expressions such as *to pass muster*, this expression emerged independently — in America in the late 1800s — and is therefore unrelated to any other turn of phrase.

One theory is that the phrase alludes to the harvesting of mustard plants and the much-admired skill or physicality of agricultural workers in trimming or collecting the plants from the field. Alternatively, perhaps this phrase alludes not to the mustard plant but to mustard seeds, which are notoriously tiny and so would be all but impossible to slice in half; someone who was able to do just that would, therefore, be especially skilled. But perhaps the most likely explanation here (not least given the era in which it first appeared) is that the reference to "mustard" is not literal but figurative.

Just as in phrases like *as keen as mustard*, the characteristic piquancy of mustard sauce has led to it being used as a familiar metaphor for anything particularly sharp, strong, or potent. If someone were not to "cut" quite so strong a figure or performance as mustard, ultimately, they would be considered sub-par or unsuccessful.

TO GRASP THE NETTLE

To grasp the nettle is to deal with a potentially tricky or problematic issue with bravery, rapidity, or boldness.

The nettle alluded to in this phrase is the common stinging nettle, *Urtica dioica*, which can cause a painful, tingling sensation on the skin of anyone or anything that happens to brush against it, even if only for a moment. Grasping a stinging nettle with the whole of your hand, therefore, might seem like a surefire way to receive an even worse nettle sting than just happening to brush past one. But ironically (according to a little bit of old British plant folklore, at least), the opposite is said to be true.

Supposedly, the reason why some people can often fearlessly collect nettles from their gardens and hedgerows without feeling too many of the plant's ill effects is that grasping nettles swiftly and boldly causes the nettle's stinging hairs to be harmlessly squashed down against the plant. If the nettle is held firmly — unlike merely brushing against the hairs' hollow tips — a person's hand can often escape being stung.

This old folkloric theory dates back to the late 16th century at least. Whether you want to test how true it is, however, is up to you!

THE WHOLE NINE YARDS

From *the whole hog* to *the whole shooting match*, and from *the whole shebang* (a shebang being a kind of Civil War soldier's hut) to *the whole nine yards*, English has a great many slang expressions beginning with "the whole..." that are all used to imply a sense of totality or completeness.

As that medley of examples above might suggest, most of these expressions appear to have been coined completely arbitrarily, and while some have stood the test of time and continue to be used today, others have doubtless fallen by the wayside as our language has developed. It's certainly possible, then, that *the whole nine yards* is little more than an arbitrary invention, and that the reference to precisely "nine yards" here is entirely random. Nonetheless, there are at least a handful of theories that claim — whether reliably or not — that this phrase does indeed refer to something specific.

One of the most inventive theories is that the "nine yards" in *the whole nine yards* refers to the length of road that can be laid using the full quantity of concrete or asphalt contained in a standard mixing truck. It's a nice idea, certainly, but the fact that this phrase has been reliably dated as far back as 1907 in America — and the first horse-drawn cement mixer was only invented in Germany in 1904 — seems to suggest otherwise.

The *Oxford English Dictionary*'s preferred explanation, ultimately, is that this phrase is rooted in an old (and possibly apocryphal) 19th-century story about a draper who requested that a

seamstress in his employ purchase three shirts' worth of fabric —
with each shirt in turn requiring roughly three yards of cloth.
When the seamstress got to work, however, she accidentally
used all nine yards of material in one single gigantic garment.

Perhaps as this anecdote or joke became better known in 19th
century America, it helped to inspire the expression *the whole
nine yards* — helped too, at least in part, by all the other
"whole..." phrases we have picked up throughout the years!

PANDORA'S BOX

Figuratively speaking, a *Pandora's box* is a place or situation comprising (or metaphorically "containing") all manner of unpleasant things. The related expression *to open Pandora's box* ultimately means to unleash all kinds of horrors and unpleasantness by "opening" or addressing just such a difficult situation.

As you likely already know, like many expressions, this one's roots lie in the myths of Ancient Greece. According to several versions of her story, Pandora was the first woman in all creation in Greek legend and was created by the divine master craftsman Hephaestus — at the behest of the king of the gods, Zeus — out of the earth.

Pandora had great beauty and all the best features of womanhood bestowed upon her by Zeus, but in revenge for the god Prometheus stealing the gift of fire from the gods and giving it to humankind, Zeus also gave Pandora a terrible curse. In her possession was a box (or, in some versions of her story, a jar) inside which were all the worst troubles and pestilences of Earth.

After she had been created, Zeus decided to send Pandora not to Prometheus himself (who was aware of his trick), but to Prometheus' brother, Epimetheus. Despite Prometheus warning him of Zeus' devilish plan, Epimetheus fell for Pandora and made her his wife. On the night of their marriage, however, Pandora snuck away from her wedding party, and overcome with curiosity, opened the box she had been given by Zeus. As a result, all the worries and troubles imaginable were unleashed upon Earth.

By the time Pandora could place the lid back on her box, however, just one thing remained inside — hope — which she then unwittingly kept from a divinely troubled humanity.

IN THE OFFING

If something is *in the offing*, then it is impending, nearby, or liable to take place in the very near future. But what exactly is "the offing"? And how exactly can you be "in" it?

Like a lot of our most curious expressions, this is an old maritime turn of phrase. In naval parlance, the offing is the more distant or furthest visible area of the sea as viewed from the shore. In this context, the English word dates back at least to the early 1600s.

A vessel that can be seen from the shore to be quite literally "in the offing" is clearly on its way to port, and so will arrive imminently. And it was from this very literal meaning that the expression *in the offing* came to be used more figuratively—of anything that is close at hand or in the near future—in the late 18th century.

PARTING SHOT

A *parting shot* is a final and especially cutting or insulting remark, often delivered in conversation or in the heat of an argument before the person delivering it departs.

As an expression in its own right, *parting shot* was originally quite literal and referred to the actual final shot, or projectile, thrown in a military assault or battle. The more figurative use of the phrase—in relation to the last cutting words thrown into a bitter argument or verbal confrontation—emerged somewhat later than the original military sense, in the mid-1800s.

There is, however, a further complication to this story that takes us back to ancient Asia. The Parthians were a race of people who lived in Parthia, a region of what is now northern Iran and southern Turkmenistan, close to the southeastern shores of the Caspian Sea. The Parthian Empire flourished for more than 500 years—from sometime around the 3rd and 2nd centuries BCE to the early 200s CE—during which time it became known for the skillfulness and expertise of its horsemen.

In particular, mounted troops in the Parthian armies became known for a bizarre battle technique in which they would feign a retreat from the battlefield, only to swivel around in their saddles as they rode away, managing to continue firing arrows at their opponents as they retreated. This baffling yet devastatingly clever ploy became known to historians as a "Parthian shot"—a term that has been recorded in English since the mid-1600s.

The similarity of *parting shot* and *Parthian shot* has led to the notion that one likely inspired the other. The Parthian shot itself is more than 2,000 years old, while the expression is almost 200 years older than the *parting shot*—all of which would suggest that it inspired the later term. That's certainly a plausible theory, yet without any textual evidence to connect the two, it may simply be the case that the similarity between these two phrases—both in meaning and form—is nothing more than a coincidence!

TO BE HOIST BY
YOUR OWN PETARD

If someone is *hoist by their own petard*, then they fall victim to their own machinations or succumb to their own hubris. But what exactly is a "petard"? And how can you be "hoist" by it?

As strange as it may sound in this context, historically a petard was a kind of simple explosive, often comprising little more than a wooden or metal box containing a fuse and a small amount of gunpowder. Due to their small size and the relatively small explosion they would therefore create, petards were often used for small-scale military and criminal purposes, such as blowing open gates and doors and creating openings in walls and other barriers. If someone were to be "hoist" — that is, thrown into the air — by their own petard, ultimately, they would be caught up in the blast of the explosive they themself planted.

The word *petard* itself was borrowed into English from French in the 1500s (and, as even stranger as it may sound, in the sense of a small explosion is distantly descended from a French word for a fart!). From there, we can skip forward a few decades to the early 1600s, when William Shakespeare first used the line "hoist with his own petard" in the third act of his masterpiece, *Hamlet*.

It was Shakespeare, then, who popularized the use of this expression in English, and it is his wording that we still use to this day.

PYRRHIC VICTORY

You might have heard the expression *Pyrrhic victory* used to describe someone or something that, although successful, still seems unhappy, is doomed ultimately to be defeated, or in some way at least appears worse off as a result of their successes.

The phrase *Pyrrhic victory* alludes to the legendary King Pyrrhus of Epirus—a coastal region of northern Ancient Greece, now close to the Greek border with Albania, over which he ruled in the 3rd and 4th centuries BCE. Crowned at the age of just 12, Pyrrhus' early rule saw the young and inexperienced king form several much-needed alliances with neighboring rulers and kingdoms, many of which he later went on to undo as an adult.

As he became older and a more experienced leader (and eventually, an increasingly despotic one!), King Pyrrhus gained a reputation for securing victory in battle with his opponents at immense material cost to his own side—hence a *Pyrrhic victory*.

In the 290s and 280s BCE, King Pyrrhus took advantage of civil unrest in nearby Macedonia to enter into fighting against his one-time ally, Demetrius I, and thereby claim several Macedonian borderlands as his own in a series of brutal and costly battles. Then, in 281 BCE, he traveled to mainland Italy with 25,000 of his men and there launched a series of devastating raids and battles against the city of Rome.

Pyrrhus' victories in Roman Europe spurred him ever onwards and eventually led to the so-called Pyrrhic Wars of 280–275 BCE. This long series of conflicts saw Pyrrhus for a time successfully extend his power even further into mainland Italy and Sicily — yet in the process, he lost many thousands of men and dozens of his warships.

In the end, despite the immediate success of his wars in Italy, the losses Pyrrhus incurred in his five years of war (as well as his increasing unpopularity among the Sicilian Greeks over which he uncompromisingly imposed his rule!) led to his eventual retreat to mainland Greece. There, he later died in fighting in the city of Argos in 272 BCE.

TO BE CUT TO THE QUICK

Although today we're more used to the word *quick* being used as an adjective meaning rapid, it can, of course, also be used as a noun. The quick is the tender, raw, and highly sensitive area of the finger that often becomes painfully exposed when you cut your nails down too low. This part of the body is so sensitive, in fact, that it is the origin of the expression *to be cut to the quick.*

We say that we are *cut to the quick* when we are especially hurtfully or brutally affected by a snide comment, a passing blow, or some similarly insignificant injury or jibe. This expression implies that such a comment stings us just as much as being "cut" down to the raw and exposed "quick" of a shortened fingernail or toenail. It is a common and well-established feeling too, as versions of this expression have been in use in English since the 16th century at least!

DEAD RINGER

A *dead ringer* is someone or something that looks (almost) exactly the same as someone or something else. But why do we call such a duplicate *a dead ringer* at all?

Popular etymology will have you believe that this phrase refers to the supposed practice of burying dead bodies with bells attached on the surface of their feet. Should the person inside the coffin not actually be dead at all but eventually regain consciousness and require to be rescued, they could wiggle their toes from six feet under and alert anyone passing by to their predicament. Folk etymologists will also have you believe that this bizarre practice is likewise the origin of being "saved by the bell."

As evocative as tales such as these are, unfortunately, there is little to back them up (and being *saved by the bell*, in fact, derives from the world of boxing, not live burials!). So, if these graveyard bells have nothing to do with dead ringers, what does?

This phrase derives from the world of horse racing. In 19th-century America, duplicitous jockeys and racehorse owners would sometimes covertly replace a horse they have entered into a race with one that looks exactly like it as a way of cheating the bookies—that is, cashing in on a poor-quality horse's long odds by swapping it out for a younger, fitter horse that looks exactly like it. This replacement horse was known as a "ringer," while the word "dead" here does not mean lifeless, but rather exact or precise (the same sense that the word has in expressions like *dead center* and *dead stop*).

A *dead ringer*, then, is not a bell, and certainly isn't dead — but is, as strange as it may seem, a horse that looks precisely like another!

TO BURY ONE'S HEAD IN THE SAND

To intentionally ignore troubling facts or to refuse to acknowledge an unpleasant reality is to *bury your head in the sand.*

This phrase's origins take us back to Ancient Rome and the curious writings of the Roman scholar and naturalist Pliny the Elder. One of the most celebrated of all Roman writers, Pliny produced a number of highly detailed research works throughout his life, including a vast 37-volume encyclopedia of all living things known as his *Natural History.*

However, as vast a work as *Natural History* is—and as keen a researcher as Pliny himself doubtless was—unfortunately, his work is oftentimes misguided, and several of his descriptions of animals and their behavior are far from accurate. It is Pliny's writings, for instance, that have led to the age-old myth that in times of trouble or when pursued by a predator, the giant desert ostrich quite literally buries its head in the sand to avoid dealing with the problem.

In truth, ostriches do nothing of the sort; instead, it seems likely that Pliny based his description of the ostrich's curious behavior on their tendency to lower their heads down to the ground to scan the horizon or to read the lay of the surrounding land. Nevertheless, Pliny's encyclopedia quickly became one of the standard research texts of Roman and later medieval Europe and so firmly established this myth in our collective consciousness that we ended up with a phrase—*to bury your head in the sand*—inspired directly by it!

TO CALL OR RIDE SHOTGUN

There's an old language myth that claims that *riding shotgun* — that is, to travel in the front passenger seat of a vehicle — comes from the days of stagecoaches in the American West when an armed guard would typically accompany a driver up in the front of a vehicle in case of attacks from bandits or outlaws.

The odd thing about this language myth, however, is that it is entirely true!

Although recorded in the language only since the early 1900s, most language historians agree that *riding shotgun* indeed derives from a time when an armed guard would be required to accompany a driver on perilous coach journeys in often treacherous or largely uncharted territory. The phrase presumably dates back to the 19th century, although evidence before the early 1900s is sadly lacking. From its original context, *riding shotgun* came to be used more generally to mean to act as a protector, before *calling shotgun* came into use in the 1960s, meaning to demand to ride in the front passenger seat before anyone else has a chance to call it for themselves.

TO GIVE SOMEONE
THE COLD SHOULDER

The cold shoulder has been a proverbial name for an unsocial rejection, or a deliberate show of indifference or unfriendliness, since the early 1800s. And in this phrase's fuller form, people have been *giving, showing,* or even *tipping the cold shoulder* at individuals toward whom they feel indifferent or apathetic since at least the 1820s. (This is an expression you'll even find used in the writings of Charles Dickens!)

As much as this sounds like this could be a fairly literal expression—perhaps referring to someone physically turning their shoulder coolly toward someone they dislike—oddly, the origins of *giving the cold shoulder* lie in the kitchen. Or rather, on the dinner table.

The "cold shoulder" you proverbially give someone when you act this way was originally and more fully the "cold shoulder of mutton"—mutton being the often tough and rather gristly meat of a mature sheep. The notion behind this phrase is therefore that an unwelcome or unpleasant guest at your dinner table would be intentionally served the worst cut of the meat by their host as a none-too-subtle sign that their presence is not wanted!

SILVER BULLET

People have been making and writing about silver bullets since the 1600s — but it is only since the mid-1900s that the expression has come to be used, as it more often is today, to refer to some manner of miraculous cure-all or solution, or else something that seemingly fixes all problems all but simultaneously. So how did this item of ammunition come to be used in this more figurative way?

As you might have guessed, the missing link here is the paranormal. Back in the day, folklore held considerably more sway over people's lives than it does today, and people still believed in monsters, ghosts, and ghouls haunting the spookiest places in the world. In those times, shooting a silver bullet at whatever supernatural threat you were supposedly dealing with was considered a surefire way of slaying it, where other weapons or projectiles would fail.

Although this method is said to have been successful in killing both witches and vampires, it is against werewolves that a silver bullet is said to have been particularly effective. Some folklorists have even pinpointed a specific case of a supposed werewolf in France in 1767 — in which a farmer is reported to have killed a ferocious dog-like beast on his land using silver bullets — as the origin of this particular superstition!

SISYPHEAN TASK

A *Sisyphean task* is a job or chore that seems unending, and in particular, a task that, just as you feel it is nearing completion, is revealed to be nowhere near over.

The adjective *Sisyphean* derives from the name of Sisyphus, a character in Greek mythology who is described as either the father of Odysseus or the father of the warrior Glaucus, as well as a crafty and avaricious king of the city-state of Corinth.

The details of Sisyphus' life not only differ from one myth to the next, so do the circumstances that led to him becoming synonymous with a thanklessly unending task. According to one story, Sisyphus witnessed the god Zeus kidnap a mortal woman in Corinth named Aegina and incurred his wrath by telling Aegina's father who was behind her disappearance in return for material wealth.

In another version of the tale, Sisyphus tells his wife that, were he to die, she should not observe the traditional funeral rites expected of a woman at that time. When Death later comes to collect Sisyphus, however, he complains to him on his arrival in the Underworld that his wife is doing him a great disservice by not holding a proper funeral and begs to be allowed back to the world of the living to chastise her. Death reluctantly agrees with Sisyphus—but once the king is allowed back up to the surface, he refuses to enter the Underworld ever again.

Sisyphus' audacity in both of these stories eventually proved his downfall. Once he is finally brought back to the Underworld, Sisyphus is punished by being made to roll a gigantic boulder up a hill for all eternity; just as the boulder reaches the top of the hill, however, it rolls down the other side and Sisyphus has to begin his eternal, exhausting task all over again.

SOUR GRAPES

When someone comes to criticize or disparage something that they might otherwise have been expected to enjoy, you might hear their grumbling words dismissed as nothing more than *sour grapes*.

It's an expression of peevish criticism that we have used in English since the mid-1700s — but its roots stretch much further back in time than that.

In fact, this is another expression we owe to the fables of the Greek writer Aesop, dating from around the 6th century BCE. In the fable of *The Fox and the Grapes*, Aesop wrote of a hungry fox who attempted to jump up and reach some grapes that were hanging from a vine. Despite his best efforts, however, the grapes were just beyond the fox's reach, and he was forced to give up his meal.

As he walked away, the fox grumbled, "Oh, I didn't even want them anyway! They're not ripe, and no one likes sour grapes…"

TO PULL OUT
ALL THE STOPS

If you *pull out all the stops,* you make every conceivable effort to do or to achieve something. But what exactly are these proverbial "stops"? Well, as odd as it may sound, at the root of this phrase is a large church organ.

If you have ever seen or played an organ yourself, you'll know that the sound made by forcing air through the organ pipes can be altered by activating a series of dials or switches that variously restrict or rechannel airflow itself. These dials are known as stops, and different combinations of them are what allow a church organ to be at times soft and doleful-sounding, and at other times brash and bombastic.

Pulling out all the stops, ultimately, would activate all of the airflow mechanisms inside the organ simultaneously, with the resulting sound being a wild medley of all manner of different tones and timbres—and it is for that reason that this expression has come to imply an equally brash, clamorous, all-out effort.

SWAN SONG

Swans are graceful birds that, among many other quirks and attributes, do not sing. They might hiss like a goose or make a raucous quacking or trumpeting like a duck, but swans are not songbirds. So why is a person's final performance known as their *swan song*?

Yet again, this is a phrase that we can ascribe to an old and rather bizarre bit of animal folklore. Although swans do not ordinarily sing, at least one particular legend claims that they produce a beautiful, haunting song the very moment that they die.

References to this myth date back to medieval times, but it wasn't until the classical and romantic periods of the 1700s and 1800s that the phrase *swan song* itself first emerged. Composers such as Robert Schumann used the phrase (or at least, its German equivalent, *Schwanengesang*) as the title of mournful vocal compositions at least in part imagined to be as haunting and as beautiful as a swan's final song. The popularity of these compositions helped to introduce the term to English, and it fell into use more generally in the language—as a byword for any farewell appearance or final performance—in the 1830s.

THE SWORD
OF DAMOCLES

When you have something worrying or unpleasant hanging over you for a long time, the constant stress can feel like *the sword of Damocles*.

According to legend, Damocles was a courtier in the employ of the tyrant king Dionysius I of Syracuse, an Ancient Greek city-state in modern-day Sicily, sometime in the 4th century BCE.

One day, Damocles was overheard talking in wild and overblown terms of what he believed to be the king's obvious happiness given his great status, power, and wealth. In response, the king invited Damocles to attend a sumptuous banquet with him in his royal hall, where Dionysius promptly sat Damocles in a chair beneath a large sharp sword that dangled above his head on nothing more than a single piece of thread. Throughout the entire meal, the sword dangled perilously above Damocles, and at any point, it could have snapped the thread and killed him immediately.

Once the meal was over, mercifully the king moved Damocles away from the sword and told him that his ordeal that day was meant as a warning: that just because he, as the king, has utmost power and wealth does not mean that he is happy, and his fortunes are just as precarious and as easily lost as those of other men.

TO FLY TOO
CLOSE TO THE SUN

To fly too close to the sun is to suffer a downfall—or else, risk failing or losing everything—as a result of your own excessive hubris or ambition.

The saying alludes to the legend of Icarus and his father, the master craftsman Daedalus (best known for being the architect of the Minotaur's labyrinth). Imprisoned together in a high tower on the island of Crete, Daedalus used his impeccable engineering skills to fashion for himself and his son two gigantic pairs of wings made of birds' feathers held together with wax. Leaping from the top of the tower, the pair flew to their escape, far out across the sea—but as they continued their flight, despite his father's warning, Icarus became overconfident and began flying ever higher, attempting to soar as high as the sun itself.

The higher and closer to the sun he flew, however, the warmer the air became and the wax in Icarus' wings began to melt. Eventually, Icarus' wings fell apart and he plummeted to his death in the sea below.

His fate—and the show of overambition that brought it on him— have since become a proverbial warning not to let your self-confidence or hubris grow too great.

STORM IN A TEACUP

A *storm in a teacup* is a great tumult or uproar made over a problem or situation that has little or no importance in the grand scheme of things.

The phrase *storm in a teacup* itself dates back to the 1800s, but different versions and wordings of this expression have existed since the 16th century at least. Among the very earliest versions to catch on, in fact, was a proverbial *storm in a cream bowl*, while Victorian writers also wrote of storms in teapots, glasses of water, wash-hand basins, and even "slop basins."

No matter how this expression is worded, however, the underlying image remains the same: something that seems like a great, tempestuous disturbance is, in reality, so insignificant that it can be entirely housed inside some manner of simple household vessel!

TO STEAL SOMEONE'S THUNDER

Some of the expressions we've looked at in this collection have been wildly inventive, relying on metaphor, myth, and allusion. Others have been far more literal — and oddly, *to steal someone's thunder* falls into this second group!

The origins of this peculiar expression take us back to 1709 and to London's theatrical West End, where the English playwright John Dennis was staging a production of his latest play, *Appius and Virginia*. The production was not a success (a "dull tragedy," as one writer later remembered it!) and closed after just four nights. Yet the play nevertheless appears to have become well known across the city for Dennis' use of special effects.

Dennis' production required making the sound of a thunderstorm, which he innovatively managed to recreate inside the theatre using a system of wooden troughs, down which heavy metal cannonballs were rolled. As the balls trundled along the troughs, they produced a loud rumbling noise that sounded exactly like thunder to those in the audience.

Not long after Dennis' short-lived play closed, he attended a performance of another play (often said to have been *Macbeth*) at another theatre in London. Midway through the production, Dennis heard a familiar sound rumbling down through the auditorium, and reportedly rose from his chair in the audience and angrily exclaimed, "Damn them!…They will not let my play run, and yet they steal my thunder!"

Dennis' outburst became proverbial in the theatrical world and soon established itself in the language in relation to someone or something stealing or taking advantage of another's work or efforts.

CAT GOT YOUR TONGUE?

When someone struggles to say something—or to even open their mouth to produce sound at all—you might hear someone jokingly ask, *"Cat got your tongue?"*

This highly bizarre expression has led to a great many equally bizarre attempts to explain it. One theory alleges that the "cat" in question here is that of a witch or sorceress, who were once well known for their ability to deprive other people of the ability to speak. Another is a far grislier explanation—namely that *cat got your tongue* refers to some curious episode in myth or ancient history in which someone's tongue was actually cut out and fed to some bloodthirsty tyrant's pet cat (perhaps, as some people would have you believe, back in the days of Ancient Egypt). A third origin theory claims that the "cat" here is not actually a feline, but the dreaded cat-o'-nine-tails—a nine-tailed scourge once used as a naval punishment to flog mutinous or undisciplined sailors.

In fact, it seems unlikely any of these explanations is true, not least given that this expression is barely a century or so old and appears to have emerged in the United States sometime in the mid-1800s (before catching on more widely in the early 20th century). Such imaginative connections to the likes of witchcraft and the cat-worshipping Ancient Egyptians, ultimately, seem highly unlikely—so perhaps instead this phrase is meant to be nothing more than a playful childhood image, along the same lines of a parent "stealing" their infant's nose by placing their thumb between their knuckles.

TO THROW IN THE TOWEL

If you *throw in the towel*, you give up on whatever enterprise or endeavor you were attempting.

Perhaps unsurprisingly, the origins of this expression—which dates back to the 1910s—lie inside a boxing ring. The rules of boxing dictate that if a fighter is experiencing a beating and seems destined to be knocked out, the support team in his or her corner can quite literally throw a towel into the ring to signal that they want the fight stopped. The phrase *throw in the towel* as we would use it today is simply a figurative extension of this boxing practice.

There is, however, an odd appendix to this story. Although *throwing in the towel* seems to date no further back than the early 20th century, before then boxing matches could be stopped by a sponge, not a towel, being tossed into the ring. As a result, *to throw up the sponge* was a mid-19th century version of this phrase, likewise used to mean to submit, or give up a concerted effort. Sadly, this older version has not stood the test of time!

ON TENTERHOOKS

Some people incorrectly pronounce this expression as "tenderhooks," perhaps under the mistaken apprehension that the stressful, edgily suspenseful situation described this way is akin to the "tender" feeling of a raw wound or injury. In fact, the actual image this phrase is meant to convey is not one of pained anxiety but of being pulled uncomfortably taut.

Since medieval times, sewers and fabric-makers have used large wooden frames known as *tenters* to stretch newly woven or dyed material so that it remains flat and square and does not become misshapen. As the fabric industry took off during the Industrial Revolution, often huge numbers of the tenter frames would be lined up in rows in large open spaces and fields, where dozens and dozens of pieces of cloth could be dried or stretched at once — and the tiny hooks or tacks that held the fabric in place on the tenters were known as tenterhooks.

The image of these vast pieces of cloth pulled tight like this is the origin of being *on tenterhooks*, in the sense that someone experiencing a stressful or suspenseful situation feels just as stretched and as wrung out as a swath of taut fabric. It is a familiar and long-standing feeling too, as people have been talking of being *put, set,* or *stretched on the tenters* since the 16th century!

COLD TURKEY

When we immediately stop doing something that has been a long-standing habit, or with which we were accustomed, why do we call it *"going cold turkey"*?

This is an expression that dates back to early-1900s America when it was first used (as it still often is today) to refer to the act of treating drug addicts by instantly cutting off their supply.

Folk etymologists will tell you that this approach became known as *cold turkey* because the cold, pimply, needle-marked skin of drug users was said to resemble that of an uncooked plucked turkey. In fact, this no-nonsense approach is tied to another, slightly older American expression: in 19th-century English, *to talk cold turkey* meant to talk straightforwardly or to get right down to business with no small talk or wasted time. No-nonsense "cold turkey" conversation or negotiation simply lent its name to no-nonsense medical treatments.

But this only solves half of the problem here. If *going cold turkey* comes from *talking cold turkey*, why were people "talking cold turkey" in the first place? Unfortunately, although a handful of theories have been proposed, that particular etymological mystery remains unsolved!

TO WAX LYRICAL

When someone speaks about something in a very enthusiastic or overblown way, they might be described as *waxing lyrical*.

Despite immediate appearances, this bizarre turn of phrase actually has nothing to do with the wax you'll find in a crayon or a candle. Instead, in this context, *to wax* means to make or become bigger and is an ancient word—found in Old English as *weaxen*—that has largely fallen out of use in English today.

In fact, *wax* in this sense is only really used in two contexts in modern English. The moon is still said to wax and wane when it builds up to and disappears from a full moon. And when people are said to *wax lyrical* about something, they are literally said to aggrandize it in flowing, lyrical prose.

The stock phrase *wax lyrical* dates from the early 20th century, but two earlier forms—to *wax eloquent* and to *wax poetic*—date back even further, into the mid-1800s.

DOWN TO THE WIRE

If a race or contest remains undecided even in its final moments, we might say that it has come right *down to the wire*.

Perhaps unsurprisingly, this expression is remarkably straightforward. The "wire," in this context, is the white tape or rope stretched across the finishing line of a race, which the winning athlete or competitor has to be the first to cross. A race that comes *down to the wire* will quite literally be decided on the finish line itself.

Dating back to the late 1800s, this expression was first used in this literal sense in relation to horse racing, before the figurative notion of something remaining undecided until its final moments emerging metaphorically in the 1920s. It is this "wire," incidentally, that also crops up in the expression *under the wire*, meaning to finish a race or complete a task or piece of work just before the time runs out.

WOLF IN SHEEP'S CLOTHING

A *wolf in sheep's clothing* is something or someone that, despite benign appearances, is a malicious or potentially deadly disguised threat.

The image at work in this phrase is a particularly ancient one, with parallels both in the Ancient Greek fables of Aesop and the New Testament. Aesop's fables predate the Gospels by several centuries, of course, so it seems his wolf was the original disguise.

Aesop's *The Wolf in Sheep's Clothing* tells of a wolf that climbs inside the skin of a sheep to hide among a flock as a means of securing an easy meal. When the shepherd arrives, however, he seizes the disguised wolf and — thinking it as just another of his livestock and looking for a meal himself — slaughters it.

Aesop's Fables were so well known in antiquity that that story would have doubtless been known to the writers of the Gospels, who wrote of "false prophets" that "come to you in sheep's clothing, but inwardly...are ravening wolves" (Matthew 7:15). Whether it was the Bible or the original morality tale that introduced this phrase to English in medieval times, however, is debatable.

TO CRY WOLF

To cry wolf is to raise a false alarm. Famously, this expression—which dates from 19th-century English—derives from a far older fairytale, the roots of which lie in yet another of the Ancient Greek writer Aesop's fables.

Aesop's story of *The Boy Who Cried Wolf* concerns a young shepherd boy who repeatedly fools people into thinking that a wolf is attacking the town's livestock. Having been fooled several times by the boy's trick, the townspeople no longer believe the boy when he cries out one final time that there is a wolf in the pasture. This time, however, there really *is* a wolf—which proceeds to devour the town's sheep (and, in some later versions of the tale, even the lying shepherd boy himself).

The moral of Aesop's original fable was that proven liars are rightly never trusted again.

AMERICANISMS

THE CATBIRD SEAT

Catbirds are predatory songbirds, similar to thrushes and shrikes, that are so called because of their noticeable mewing-like call. Their characteristically brash temperament—catbirds are known for attacking and intimidating other birds in their territory—has led to their name long being used as a metaphor for any similarly powerful or authoritarian person, especially one who uses their position to browbeat others. But where does that leave the curious expression *catbird seat*?

In recorded use since the 1940s, the *catbird seat* is a phrase used to describe a lofty, privileged, or advantageous position. At least partly inspired by the name of a James Thurber short story, "The Catbird Seat," which was published in *The New Yorker* in 1942, the phrase alludes to the catbird's habit of taking the very highest perch possible—typically at the very top of a tall tree—and using its position to look down on the surrounding territory and from there hunt its prey of small rodents, frogs, and lizards.

TO HAVE BOUGHT
THE FARM

A turn of phrase little heard outside the United States, if you have *bought the farm* then you have died — or, more often than not in this context, been killed.

To buy it has been a slangy expression meaning to die since the days of World War I and is still heard on occasion in English today. Perhaps inspired by that, in the 1940s and 50s, post-war aircraftmen taking new aircraft on test flights in remote locations would sometimes suffer mechanical problems and be forced to crash land on whatever large, wide-open space they could find — more often than not, a farmer's field.

The crash understandably tended to take the life of the poor pilot on board, as well as cause untold damage to the farmer's crop. And as the military was ultimately to blame for the accident, the farmer could sue the US government for compensation, typically receiving more than enough cash in return to buy his farm and his land outright.

The pilot at the center of the accident, therefore, could be said to have "bought the farm" with his life.

TO TAKE THE CAKE

If something or someone *takes the cake*, then they have, in some form, won—claiming a prize, claiming honors, or in some way taking first place in the process.

This phrase dates back to the mid-1800s and was originally used in the plural; as far back as 1839, winning parties were said to *take the cakes*, not just the cake. There is some disagreement over precisely what this phrase implied, however, but a likely explanation is that the cake or cakes involved were quite literally prizes awarded for a first-place position. In that sense, some historians have proposed that the phrase might have originated among so-called "cakewalking" shows and competitions held among Black communities in the 19th and early 20th centuries.

One problem with that explanation, however, is the existence of a whole host of alternative versions of this phrase. *Take the cake* might be the first of these, but throughout the 1800s and 1900s, all manner of different treats and prizes were being proverbially "taken" by someone who had excelled. British English today, for instance, still prefers the phrase *take the biscuit*, while versions as varied as *taking the bakehouse*, *taking the bakery*, *taking the gingerbread*, *taking the teacake*, and even *grabbing the currant bun* have all been recorded.

Rather than referring to a specific prize-giving cakewalk, ultimately, perhaps this phrase—and the countless versions of it that have been in use over the decades—is simply based on the winning party being rewarded with any kind of proverbial treat!

TO EAT CROW

To eat crow is to eat humble pie — that is, to recognize that you have made a mistake and be forced or compelled to admit as such.

Crow meat is, of course, an undesirable and fairly meager meal, so perhaps the image underpinning this expression is nothing more than the unpleasantness of the image itself. There is, however, an alternative theory that this expression derives from a genuine episode from American history in which a British officer during the War of 1812 came across an American soldier who had shot a crow on British land. Presumably wanting to impress his power and status onto the soldier, the officer forced the American to eat (at least part of) the crow he had killed.

Whether that tale is true or not, this bizarre play on eating humble pie certainly did emerge — first in American English — in the early 19th century.

As for humble pie itself, meanwhile, that derives from *umbles pie*, a medieval-era name for a pastry dish consisting of offal and other rather dubious meat offcuts.

TO EIGHTY-SIX

Why does *to eighty-six* (or even *to 86*) mean to throw something out, reject something, cancel it, or even—in some contexts, at least—to die or be killed?

At the root of this curiosity of American English is rhyming slang—a jargonish form of language in which commonly used words or phrases are playfully replaced with an often random word or phrase that just so happens to rhyme. In this case, *eighty-six* replaced the existing word *nix*, or *nyx*, meaning to cancel. (Nix itself, incidentally, is an ancient Germanic word literally meaning "nothing" and is a distant relative of the word *nought.*)

It is thought that it was in the barrooms and cafeterias of early 1900s America that nix was first playfully replaced by the number 86 (though why that was chosen as a rhyme instead of anything else is a complete mystery!). From there, the term quickly caught on in American parlance but has yet to find much use elsewhere in the English-speaking world.

FULL-COURT PRESS

A *full-court press* is an extreme and utterly determined offensive or effort to do something.

The phrase itself comes from the world of basketball, where it was first used in the 1940s to refer to a defensive tactic employed during a game in which the defenders attempt to pile pressure on their opponents across the entire court, thereby disrupting their ability to work with one another and easily play the game to their advantage.

The phrase was introduced to the sport in 1940s, but it was in the later 20th century that *full-court press* first came to be used more broadly and more figuratively to refer to any such all-out effort, regardless of its context.

INDIAN GIVER

In the 18th and 19th centuries, the tensions between Native Americans and both European colonists and new American citizens were very high. As a result, the native peoples found themselves on the receiving end not only of violence but also linguistic scorn and opprobrium.

Indian giver — a term for someone who gives a gift and then asks for it back — is an expression that dates from this uneasy period in American history. Although some attempts to explain the term have attached stories of specific exchanges between Native Americans and Europeans to it, these are likely apocryphal. Instead, the term seems to have been coined simply because the behavior it alludes to is considered rude and is looked down upon, just as the native peoples were at the time it was invented. There was, moreover, an earlier expression, an *Indian gift*, used to refer to what one 18th-century writer described as "a present for which an equivalent return is expected."

Another theory is that the phrase emerged from Native American peoples' generously lending tools, equipment, medicine, or other such useful items to the Europeans and settlers as they pushed America's borders ever westward — with the Europeans misunderstanding the situation, presuming the loans were gifts, and therefore being bemused when the native peoples asked for their items back!

YOUR JOHN HANCOCK

Your John Hancock—or more simply, just *your Hancock*—is your signature.

It should perhaps come as little surprise that this is a phrase little used outside of the United States of America, given that it refers to an aspect of perhaps the most quintessentially American of documents.

The real John Hancock was one of the earliest major statesmen of colonial Massachusetts and a leading figure during America's Revolutionary War. Elected state governor in 1780, he then served in Congress under the *Articles of Confederation* in 1785, eventually going on to become the longest-serving president of the Continental Congress in its history. And it was during his presidency of the Continental Congress that the *American Declaration of Independence* was drawn up, adopted, and signed. In John Trumbull's famous 1826 painting of the signing of the declaration, in fact, it is Hancock who is seen being presented with the final wording of the document by Thomas Jefferson.

As president of the Continental Congress, Hancock was the first person to sign the *Declaration of Independence*. And as there were no other names on the document at that time, understandably, Hancock signed his name rather largely and rather prominently, in the very center of the open space at the bottom of the text. As more signatories' names were added, however, they were forced to write their names rather smaller to leave room for everyone else.

Hancock's name ended up being the largest and most obviously visible name of all the signatories of the *Declaration of Independence*—and as the document's appearance became more widely known, his prominent name became a byword for anyone's signature in the late 1800s.

MONDAY MORNING QUARTERBACK

If you're a sports fan, chances are you'll have heard the expression *Monday morning quarterback* on more than a few occasions.

The term refers to someone who second-guesses the decisions of other people or their own previous confidences or knowledge. More broadly, it is often used to describe someone who fails to realize that their criticisms or professed knowledge of a situation are actually based on hindsight—and if they had been in the same situation as those they are criticizing, without the benefit of later experience or insight, they too would likely have made the same decisions they're now rehashing and disagreeing with!

The term alludes to football fans and other sports fans who critically dissect the teamplay and in-game decisions of their favorite sports teams after the weekend's games are over on Monday morning. Other versions of this expression, which dates back to the 1930s, include a *Saturday night quarterback* and a *Sunday morning quarterback*; no matter how it is expressed, however, it is the notion of having wisdom *after* the fact that underpins it!

TO NICKEL AND
DIME SOMEONE

Dating back to the 1910s, the phrase *to nickel and dime someone* is often used to mean to quibble with them over small change or low-cost items—like the friend who refuses to split a restaurant bill down the middle, despite their share of the meal being only a dollar or two less than everyone else's!

Understandably, the phrase derives from the relatively low value of nickel and dime coins. However, to *nickel and dime* can also be used more broadly or more loosely to mean to get by on little cash, to annoy or badger someone (especially over something trivial), to only eke out a living or survive on a small wage, or even to beg for cash on the street.

The phrase has become so established in American vernacular, in fact, that *nickel-and-dime* can even be used as an adjective too, not merely as a verb, describing someone or something that appears insignificant or petty. Since the late 1930s, meanwhile, a *nickel-and-dimer* has been a slang term in US parlance for a mean, miserly, or similarly insignificant person.

THE PEANUT GALLERY

The very topmost tiers of seats in a theatre have been known (somewhat contemptuously) as the *peanut gallery* since the 1850s in American slang. More loosely, the phrase can also be applied to any area of especially cheap seating in a spectator's area—or in reference to the kinds of people typically reckoned to take these poor-quality seats, a group of unwanted critics or pundits who heckle from the sidelines or give unwanted advice or commentary.

The gallery in a theatre is, of course, the uppermost area of the seats (also playfully known as "the gods"), which often contains the auditorium's cheapest seating given the rather restrictive view it tends to afford. The reference to peanuts, meanwhile, refers to their being commonly sold in 19th-century theatres and music halls; due to their cheapness, peanuts were apparently the snack of choice for those in the hall's least expensive seats— hence, the entire area became known as the *peanut gallery*.

STOOL PIGEON

As well as being a word for a tall or small chair, 19th-century hunters knew a *stool* to be a makeshift portable perch to which a pigeon could be fastened as a lure for wild birds. The hapless bird involved served as a decoy, duping the other birds into thinking the area within the hunter's shooting range or trapping net was safe. Ultimately, it became known as a *stool pigeon*.

It is from this phrase's use in relation to this hunting technique that by the 1820s, *stool pigeon* had come to be used more broadly for anyone or anything that likewise acts as a decoy—unwittingly lulling others around them into thinking they can be trusted.

By the 1850s, the word had come to be used more specifically for a criminal police informant or spy, in particular one who operates in disguise or undercover, infiltrating criminal networks and reporting back what they know to their superiors.

TO TAKE A RAINCHECK

If you *take a raincheck* on something, it means you either don't accept an invitation right away or else reluctantly cancel plans you have made or fail to meet an obligation you have arranged, with the intention of rearranging them for a later, more suitable date.

The word *raincheck* or *rain check* itself dates back to the mid-1880s. Originally, it referred to an actual check or ticket stub given out to a spectator of a baseball game that had been interrupted by—or had to have been canceled or rescheduled because of—a downpour of rain. This check typically either operated as a refund of the ticket price, allowed the spectator to return to the rescheduled game, or granted them admission to another game at the same ground played at a later date.

It was based on this rather literal scenario that the phrase *taking a raincheck* first emerged in a broader and more figurative sense—referring to any canceled or deferred plans—around the turn of the last century. First recorded in 1899, the phrase has remained in use ever since in American English but remains little used outside of North America.

I SAY IT'S SPINACH

An American phrase seldom heard today, *I say it's spinach* — or more fully, "I say it's spinach, and I say the hell with it!" — was a slangy idiom popular in American English from the late 1920s onwards.

The phrase derives directly from a popular *New Yorker* cartoon that proved a surprise hit on its publication on December 8, 1928. The image, by cartoonist Carl Rose and memorably captioned by the author EB White, showed a young girl sitting at a dinner table with her well-to-do mother, with a plate of food before each of them. "It's broccoli, dear," the mother is apparently saying, to which her indignant daughter stubbornly replies, "I say it's spinach, and I say the hell with it."

The cartoon — which is often singled out as a quintessential example of *The New Yorker*'s subtle and esoteric style of humor — quickly proved a sensation, and the caption promptly fell into broader use in the language as a popular way of saying that something was false, nonsense, or poor quality.

The fad reached a pinnacle in 1932 when the great American songwriter Irving Berlin wrote a track called "I Say It's Spinach (And the Hell with It)" for his hit musical *Face the Music* (co-written with the playwright Moss Hart).

23-SKIDOO

For over a century, *23-skidoo!* (also spelled *skiddoo!*) has been variously used in American slang to order someone to leave — and, in particular, to leave as quickly as possible.

The origins of the phrase are as mysterious and as curious as the phrase itself sounds. What makes them even more curious is that it apparently represents the coming together of two separate turn-of-the-last-century expressions, both of which independently meant "get out!"

The older of the two appears to be *23*, or *twenty-three*, which first began to be used in this way in the 1890s. Quite where the phrase emerged from is unclear, with various theories suggesting it comes from the scoring system of an old gambler's dice game, refers to the maximum number of horses in a horse race, derives from the address of New York's Flatiron Building (which, rather dubiously, was not completed until after this expression had fallen into use!), or has even been lifted from the closing scenes of Charles Dickens' novel *A Tale of Two Cities*. As he is selflessly led to the guillotine in place of the husband of the woman he loves, the novel's hero, Sidney Carton, is called up to the platform not by his name, but by a number — 23.

Whether Dickens, dice, horses, New York City, (or, for that matter, some other origin story!) are responsible for entering this number into American slang remains unclear. The origin of *skidoo*, or *skiddoo*, however, is more straightforward: it is likely nothing more than a playful alteration of the older word *skedaddle*, which had by that point been in use in English for many years.

One question remains here, though: why were two separate phrases meaning "go away" — namely, *23* and *skidoo* — joined together? Some versions of this tale credit a 1904 musical play, *Little Johnny Jones*, with popularizing this expression, as it includes a line in which both phrases are used in quick succession. But a more plausible idea is that as two of the most popular buzzwords of the time, people naturally ran these two together themselves, in much the same way we might hear someone say, "See ya! Adios! Sayonara! You're outta here!" today.

BRITISHISMS

TO TAKE THE BISCUIT

While American English speakers like *to take the cake*, British English speakers tend instead *to take* or *cop the biscuit*.

As a British English speaker will no doubt attest, this biscuit is not the same as the savory biscuits typically served with gravy in parts of the United States. Those doughy masses of bread are more akin to a traditional British savory scone, or even a stewed meat dumpling. British biscuits, instead, are closer in equivalence to American cookies—and so in both this phrase and its American *cake* equivalent, the underlying notion is of someone winning a sweet treat as a reward for an exceptionally good performance.

If something *takes the biscuit*, ultimately, then it beats all rivals or expectations or secures victory in a dazzlingly impressive way. The phrase is also sometimes used to describe something or someone whose success is even more startling (or, with a more sarcastic edge, more horrendous or unwanted!) than could ever have been anticipated.

AS THE ACTRESS
SAID TO THE BISHOP

If ever there were a prize for the most quintessentially British expression, perhaps it should go to this saucily witty line, which dates back to the early 1900s.

As the actress said to the bishop is used as a tagline in British slang to turn something that has just been said in all innocence into a saucy innuendo. "Let's get down to business," one person might say, before the other adds—merely for a joke—"As the actress said to the bishop!"

If that answers how this phrase is deployed in British English, however, what about where it comes from? Why mention an actress and a bishop?

Oddly, expressions based on the format *as the X said to the Y* have been in recorded use in British English since the 1500s, with one the earliest and most curious yet to be discovered—namely, "as the rat-trap maker said to the parson"—dating back as far as 1661. Phrases like these haven't always been used to make innuendos, nor have they always been used as saucy, jocular taglines; originally, they were typically used merely to introduce a well-known proverb, saying, or everyday stock phrases, seemingly for no other reason than to give an ascription or a little more credence to it. It was in the 1930s that *as the X said to the Y* first began to be used in ruder and more bawdy circumstances in particular, no doubt urged on by the popularity of the music hall comedians and rambunctious entertainers of the interwar era.

121

Why *actress* and *bishop*, then? Perhaps only to make an already saucy joke even saucier.

TO PULL A BLINDER

If a British person *pulls* or *plays a blinder*, then they do an exceptional job or have success in something in an overtly impressive way.

The word *blinder* has been in use in British slang since the early 1800s. Back then, it initially meant a stout blow to the head or face—just the kind of assault that might (even only temporarily, at least) cause someone's eyesight to be blinded. In the later 1800s, however, the phrase *to pull* or *play a blinder* fell into use in British and Australian sports slang, referring to a game or individual play that is especially skillful or impressive.

The connection between the two meanings is likely figurative—in the sense that the play being described is so impressive that a person is temporarily blinded by its excellence (in much the same way that we might describe our mind being boggled by something particularly brilliant). Or, oppositely, this meaning may have emerged from the notion of a player being struck, tackled, or somehow hit by a "blinder" midway through a game or match, with their opponent's play not only proving successful but knocking them out in the process.

Whether literal or metaphorical, in British slang, those who perform well have been said to have *played a blinder* since long before the turn of the last century.

BOB'S YOUR UNCLE!

"If you just do that, then do this next, Bob's your uncle!"

To anyone not familiar with this characteristically British turn of phrase, hearing someone say something like that line above might be utterly befuddling. To a seasoned British English speaker, however, that exchange would make perfect sense.

Bob's your uncle is an expression used in British English to effectively mean "there you go!", "that's all you need!", "and that's alright!" — often with the added implication that what has been done (or all that is required to be done) is easy. Given that this phrase is not tied down to any particular context, moreover, *Bob's your uncle!* is an immensely varied phrase that could essentially be used any time you might otherwise say, "and that's that!", "voila!", or "ta-da!"

But who exactly was the eponymous Uncle Bob? Unfortunately, the origins of this phrase are shrouded in mystery, and other than the fact that it appears to have first come into vogue in the 1930s, no one has ever gotten to the bottom of it. One theory, however, is that the Bob in question here is none other than Robert Gascoyne-Cecil — the 3rd Marquess of Salisbury and a three-time prime minister of the United Kingdom.

The Marquess of Salisbury's three premierships lasted a total of 13 years, 1885–86, 1886–1892, and lastly 1895–1902. British politics was in such a tumultuous state at that time that Salisbury was twice preceded and twice succeeded by the same person, his archrival William Gladstone.

During his time as prime minister, the Marquess of Salisbury oversaw much of the Boer Wars and dealt with the death of Queen Victoria in 1901. But besides witnessing one of the greatest era shifts in British history, Salisbury was also known for his notorious tendency to give high-ranking positions to his friends and relatives. As a result, when he stepped down from his role as prime minister for the final time, in 1902, he handed the reins of power to his nephew, Arthur Balfour.

Given that the expression *Bob's your uncle!* appears to have emerged in British English just a matter of years later, it is certainly plausible that it was inspired by the Marquess of Salisbury's tendency to keep things in his family and the relative ease with which his nephew and successor rose to power.

TO HAVE A BUTCHER'S

One of the most inventive and unusual aspects of British English is the importance of rhyming slang — and in particular, London's Cockney rhyming slang — in establishing new words and meanings in the British vernacular. And this peculiar expression is just one of them.

In early 20th-century rhyming slang, a look was a *butcher's hook*. When a British English speaker *has* or *takes a butcher's* at something, they take a quick look or glance at it.

Rhyming slang is also responsible for archetypical Britishisms like *brassic*, meaning penniless (from *boracic lint*, a kind of medical dressing, which rhymes with *skint*, meaning broke) and *grass*, meaning a police informer (which comes from *grasshopper*, meaning either a copper or a "shopper" who gives or "shops" their secrets to the police).

A British person might also call someone up on the *dog and bone* (telephone), refer to their head as their *loaf* (as head rhymes with "loaf of bread"), tell *porkies* (i.e. pork pies, rhyming with lies), and complain about the pain in their *plates of meat* (feet) or their *Hampstead Heath* (teeth).

COCK AND BULL STORY

A *cock and bull story* is an unlikely, fanciful, or unbelievable tale.

A popular tale in British folklore alleges that this expression refers to two coaching inns, The Cock and The Bull, which operated in close proximity to one another on one of the main arterial roads, Watling Street (now England's A5 motorway), leading to and from London. The two inns' good-natured rivalry led to many an overblown tale of landlords trying to outdo the other, which ultimately gave rise to many a "Cock and Bull" story.

As intriguing a story as this is, however, it appears to be little more than a myth. Instead, labeling an unbelievable tale as *cock and bull* appears to have been inspired by an older French expression, *coq-a-l'âne* (essentially, "a cockerel and an ass"), which one 17th-century dictionary of the language defined as an "incoherent story, passing from one subject to another."

It seems likely this phrase, in turn, was inspired by the many myths, legends, and ancient fables of Europe that often featured anthropomorphized animals and other magical creatures.

LIKE THE CURATE'S EGG

The phrase "like the curate's egg" is not heard much in British English today, but it refers to something simultaneously good and bad, or that has good points and bad points intermingled together.

The phrase derives from a quintessentially Victorian witticism about manners that first appeared in print in England in 1895. Although various versions of the joke abound, the scenario always tends to involve a timid young church curate having breakfast with his superior, the bishop of his diocese. As they eat, the bishop notices that the curate's hard-boiled eye has gone off—but not wanting to cause a scene in front of the bishop, the curate continues eating it. "Dear me," the bishop exclaims, "I'm afraid your egg's not good!" To which the curate replies, "Oh no, my Lord," as he chokes down another mouthful of spoiled food. "I assure you, parts of it are excellent!"

This brief comedy of manners was then widely circulated in London's *Punch* magazine, in which it was used as the caption to a cartoon drawn by the artist George Du Maurier in November 1985. Du Maurier's image, and the witty commentary on Britishness and churchly manners that it entailed, proved popular, and *"like the curate's egg – good in parts"* soon established itself in Victorian and Edwardian English as a standard response to something found to be not all good, but not all bad either.

TO DINE WITH
DUKE HUMPHREY

Another Britishism to have long fallen out of use is this curious expression, which dates back to Tudor times. *To dine with Duke Humphrey* is to skip a meal and have no food whatsoever.

The Duke Humphrey in question here is popularly said to be the "Good Duke" Humphrey of Lancaster, the Duke of Gloucester and the youngest son of Henry IV, who lived in the 14th and 15th centuries. After his death in 1447, it was popularly believed that Humphrey was buried in St. Paul's Cathedral in London. Although he was, in fact, buried some miles away from there (in the market town of St. Albans), the popular belief held firm. The passageway beside what was reckoned to be the Good Duke's resting place became a place of refuge for beggars and paupers — those who could not guarantee the source of their next meal.

A further twist on this tale claims that the passage beside the duke's supposed tomb, known as Duke Humphrey's Walk, might also once have run down to the cathedral's refectory, and so those who gathered there might have had the added incentive of being given leftovers or scraps by the monks and clergymen who walked by.

HOBSON'S CHOICE

If you're given *Hobson's choice*, then you're given no choice at all — you will either take what you're given or go without.

This phrase, which despite its age remains in use in British English today, dates back to the 17th century. According to legend, the "Hobson" in question was a Cambridge businessman from the Tudor period named Thomas Hobson, who ran a thriving horse rental business from his stables in the city. Hobson's business — which is said to have mainly rented horses out to the students at nearby Cambridge University — had just one rule: customers could not choose the horse they wanted, but only take whichever animal was closest to the door. It was this first come, first served — (first in, first out) approach to his business that supposedly made Hobson's name synonymous with a lack of choice.

How real that tale is (and indeed, how truly uncompromising Thomas Hobson's business practices were) remains something of a mystery, however, and language historians continue to debate this explanation.

TO HAVE A MONK ON

Although recorded in print no further back than the 1980s, *to have a monk on* is a Yorkshire dialect expression that has gradually fallen into wider use in British English over the past few decades—and so was likely in use locally and in spoken English far earlier than the current written record might suggest.

The expression itself means to be in a sullen, sulky, or angry mood or to have a surly, ill-tempered look on your face. If a British English speaker *has a monk on*, ultimately, they are in bad humor and are probably best left alone!

The origins of this phrase are unclear, but two popular theories have been put forward. One claims that the "monk" in *to have a monk on* is quite literally a monk—in which case, this phrase might refer to the sullen reluctance to speak to a person in a bad mood, likened in this case to a monk who has taken a vow of silence. Alternatively, another theory claims that this might not be a monk at all, but a monkey; tellingly, the phrase *to put someone's monkey up* (in allusion to the wild behavior of the animals themselves) has been used to mean to annoy or enrage someone in British English since the 1800s.

ALL MOUTH AND
NO TROUSERS

Dating back to the mid-1900s, someone described as being *all mouth and no trousers* is full of boastful yet ultimately empty talk. In other words, they put on a big, brash, bold show — yet all their projected bravado and confidence is, in reality, non-existent.

The image here is understandably that of someone who can talk a good game (the "mouth"), but when the time comes to actually get ready to do what they claim to be able to do (the "trousers"), they are found to be decidedly lacking.

Although this version of the phrase has been dated by the *Oxford English Dictionary* to 1961, it seems likely that *all mouth and no trousers* was at least based in part on one of any number of earlier expressions of a similar vein, which likewise follow the *all X and (no) Y* template. An earlier almost identical form, "all teeth and no trousers," has been unearthed in the language as far back as 1955, while even the Victorians got in on the act with a similar expression of empty pomposity, "all gas and gaiters," dated back as far as 1856.

GONE PEAR-SHAPED

If something has *gone pear-shaped*, then it has gone awry.

According to the *Oxford English Dictionary*, this phrase appears to have been first used by Royal Air Force (RAF) pilots, before falling into wider use in the 1990s. If that is the case, there is likely a connection here to an earlier expression, *to play it pear-shaped*. That was slang used by RAF pilots since the 1960s to mean either to commit to a single course of action or else to take things easy and go with the flow. Perhaps, then, it is the tendency of easy-going, unplanned things to go awry—or else the lack of alternative options if a person steadfastly follows only a single course of action—that ultimately led to this phrase coming to describe failed or unsuccessful enterprises.

One question remains, however: why *pear-shaped*? Although several theories have been proposed (including the highly inventive notion that this phrase was, in fact, first used by glass-blowers to describe failed spherical bulbs), it may simply be the case that the oddly bowed and bottom-heavy shape of a pear is here being used as a metaphor for anything ill-formed or ultimately undesirable.

TO SPEND A PENNY

To spend a penny is to go to the toilet.

Dating back at least to the mid-1900s, *spend a penny* is used in several English-speaking nations—including Australia and Ireland—but remains most current in British English, where it has been in recorded use since the early 1940s.

Back then, the cost of using a public convenience was typically one pence, and entry into public restrooms was often achieved by placing a single old-style penny into a coin-operated turnstile or door. As a result, a person needing to use the toilet while out in public would quite literally have to spend a penny to do so!

TAKE A SHUFTI

Much like taking a butcher's, if a British English person *takes a shufti* or a *shufty* at something, then they have a look at it or take a quick glance over it.

Unlike taking a butcher's, however, *shufti* is not a word British English owes to rhyming slang. Instead, as its fairly unconventional spelling might suggest, *shufti* is a word that English picked up from overseas.

First recorded in military slang, it is thought that British army servicemen likely picked up the word *shufti* while serving in Egypt and North Africa during World War II. As such, the word is likely derived from the local Arabic phrase *sufti*, meaning "have you seen?" (or literally, "you saw").

From there, the word was taken back to England after the war and quickly fell into broader non-military use, eventually inspiring the stock phrase *take a shufti*. It has been in recorded use in English since the early 1940s.

IT DOES EXACTLY WHAT
IT SAYS ON THE TIN

If something *does exactly what it says on the tin*, then it does precisely and uncompromisingly exactly what it was expected to do or what it promised to do—often with the added implication that it does no more and no less or that it does it so well it does not need to be celebrated or pointed out.

Up to now in this collection of Britishisms, we've encountered words and phrases from wartime slang and rhyming slang and even taken a trip back to the ancient Tudor period. But this last entry has a different and far more up-to-date origin story: *exactly what it says on the tin* derives from a television commercial.

In the mid-1990s, the Yorkshire-based paint and wood stain company Ronseal began a series of advertisements on British television in which certain products were shown and uncompromisingly said to do "exactly what they say on the tin." A product for staining fence panels, for instance, would be advertised by having someone use it on screen before the pithy slogan would further hammer the message home that this was all the product did—and seemingly because it does it so well, the advertisement did not need to do or show anything else.

The slogan was first used in 1994 and proved so effective and so memorable that it quickly caught on in the British viewership's vernacular. Before long, anything that did precisely what it was meant to or promised to do was likewise being said "to do exactly what it says on the tin."

The phrase remains in use by the company today, and despite falling into wider use has since been trademarked in advertising contexts. That has not stopped other companies from parodying and even piggybacking on Ronseal's success, however, with one toothpaste company in particular advertising their product as doing "exactly what it says on the tube"!

CONCLUSION

From Ancient Greece to 21st-century film and television—by way of the likes of William Shakespeare, *The Declaration of Independence*, Charles Dickens, Queen Victoria, Irving Berlin, and even Harry Truman—we've been on quite a wild journey through these chapters and pages.

Along the way here, we've looked at more than 100 different English phrases, local idioms, wise proverbs and adages, bizarre expressions, and curious sayings, covering all the corners of the English-speaking globe and all the centuries in which our extraordinary language has been in existence.

And perhaps what has become the most obvious aspect among all of these intriguing turns of phrase and twists of linguistic history is that the English language is nothing if not adaptable, unpredictable, and utterly whimsical.

Throughout history, we English speakers have gamely picked up sayings from the Old and New Testaments, the Greek myths, and the ancient stories and fables of antiquity.

We've adopted phrases from some of our favorite and most celebrated authors, playwrights, and poets. And we've repeatedly turned to sport, games, gambling, cards, science, books, theatre, art, and natural history for inspiration.

We've recycled the names of true figures from history— including politicians, statesmen, kings, and queens—as well as a great many more from local folklore, myths, and legends. We've carried on using Old English and medieval words long after their first appearance in our vocabularies, passing their use down through the centuries like a linguistic heirloom, so that the phrases in which they appear today remain their only surviving use.

And even then, when all else has failed, we've just gone to a baseball game, looked at a cartoon in a newspaper, listened to a hit song or stage show, or even just turned on the television to pick up brand-new additions to our language those ways too.

All told, our language (and, for that matter, we English speakers) appears to be such a relentless sponge of new material—taking new elements and turns of phrase from every conceivable angle and source—that where it will go next and what phrases we might adopt in the future, surely cannot be predicted.

Will we continue raiding the ancient past for inspiration? Will more quotes from Shakespeare or Dickens find their way into our everyday language as we continue to read and appreciate their work? Or will film and television—and now even the internet and social media—prove the next hotbed of inventive new phrases and expressions? We're already seeing words and idioms leap out of tweets and memes, so perhaps that next stage has already begun!

Wherever our language takes us in the years to come, however, the fact that we have already covered more than 1,000 years of the history of the English language in this book—and have brought things right up to date with several entries from the 21st century—proves that English is set to be just as varied, just as haphazard, and just as interesting in the future.

Made in the USA
Las Vegas, NV
07 May 2025